AN ANTHOLOGY OF LEGENDS AND POEMS OF ARMENIA

Zabelle C. Boyajian

Aram Raffi

With special introduction by James Bryce

IndoEuropean
Publishing

CONTENTS

Armenia: Its Epics, Folk-Songs, and Mediaeval Poetry, by Aram Raffi

PREFACE

In preparing this book of Armenian Legends and Poems my principal object was to publish it as a Memorial to an unhappy nation.

The book does not claim to represent Armenian poetry adequately. Many gifted and well-known authors have been omitted, partly from considerations of space, and partly because of the scope of the work. For instance, I should have liked to include some of the Sharakans (rows of gems) of Nerses Shnorhali; but the impossibility of reproducing their characteristic forms in another language, and doing them any justice, made me decide not to translate any of them. I have only given a few typical legends and poems, endeavoring, as far as possible, to convey the local coloring by adhering closely to the form, rhythm, and imagery of the originals in my translations.

Should this anthology create an interest in Armenian literature the Armenian Muses have still many treasures in their keeping which cannot be destroyed; and another volume could be compiled.

In conclusion, I wish to express my sincerest gratitude to Miss Alice Stone Blackwell, of Boston, U.S.A.—one of Armenia's truest friends—for allowing me to reprint several of her renderings of Armenian poems; to G. C. Macaulay, M.A., and the Delegates of the Oxford University Press, for permission to reprint the "Tale of Rosiphelee" from their edition of Gower's Confessio Amantis;

to Mr. William Watson and Mr. John Lane for permission to reprint the sonnet on Armenia, "A Trial of Orthodoxy," from The Purple East.

ZABELLE C. BOYAJIAN

INTRODUCTION

SEVERED for many centuries from Western Europe by the flood of Turkish barbarism which descended upon their country in the Middle Ages, and subjected for the last two generations to oppressions and cruelties such as few civilized people have ever had to undergo, the Armenians have been less known to Englishmen and Frenchmen than their remarkable qualities and their romantic history deserve. Few among us have acquired their language, one of the most ancient forms of human speech that possess a literature. Still fewer have studied their art or read their poetry even in translations. There is, therefore, an ample field for a book which shall present to those Englishmen and Frenchmen, whose interest in Armenia has been awakened by the sufferings to which its love of freedom and its loyalty to its Christian faith have exposed it, some account of Armenian art and Armenian poetical literature. Miss Boyajian, the authoress of this book, is the daughter of an Armenian clergyman, whom I knew and respected during the many years when he was British Vice-Consul at Diarbekir on the Tigris. She is herself a painter, a member of that group of Armenian artists some of whom have, like Aivazovsky and Edgar Chahine, won fame in the world at large, and she is well qualified to describe with knowledge as well as with sympathy the art of her own people.

That art has been, since the nation embraced Christianity in the fourth century of our era, chiefly ecclesiastical. The finest examples of ancient Armenian architecture are to be seen in the ruins of Ani, on the border where Russian and Turkish territory meet, a city which was once the seat of one of the native dynasties, while the famous church of the monastery of Etchmiadzin, at Vagarshabad, near Yerevan, is, though more modern, a perfect and beautiful existing representative of the old type. Etchmiadzin, standing at the north foot of Mount Ararat, is the seat of the Catholicos, or ecclesiastical head of the whole Armenian Church. There was little or no ecclesiastical sculpture, for the Armenian Church discouraged the use of images, and fresco painting was not much used for the decoration of churches; missals, however, and other books of devotion and manuscripts of the Bible were illuminated with hand paintings, and adorned with miniatures; and much skill and taste were shown in embroideries. Metal work, especially in silver and in copper, has always been a favorite vehicle for artistic design in the Near East and is so still, though like everything else it has suffered from the destruction, in repeated massacres, of many of the most highly skilled artificers.

One of the most interesting features in the history of Armenian art is that it displays in its successive stages the various influences to which the country has been subject. Ever since it became Christian it was a territory fought for by diverse empires of diverse creeds. As in primitive times it lay between Assyria on the one side and the Hittite power on the other, so after the appearance of Islam it became the frontier on which the East Roman Christian Empire contended with the Muslim Arab and Turkish monarchies. Persian influences on the East, both before and after Persia had become Mohammedan, here met with the Roman influences spreading out from Constantinople. The latter gave the architectural style, as we see it in those ecclesiastical buildings to which I have referred, a style developed here with admirable features of its own and one which has held its ground to the present day. The influence of Persia on the other hand was seen in the designs used in embroidery, in carpets, and in metal work. The new school of painters has struck out new lines for itself, but while profiting by whatever it has learnt from Europe, it retains a measure of distinctive national quality.

That quality is also visible in Armenian poetry of which this volume gives some interesting specimens. The poetry of a people

2

which has struggled against so many terrible misfortunes has naturally a melancholy strain. But it is also full of an inextinguishable patriotism. Those who have learnt from this book what the Armenian race has shown itself capable of doing in the fields of art and literature, and who have learnt from history how true it has been to its Christian faith, and how tenacious of its national life, will hope that the time has now at last come when it will be delivered from the load of brutal tyranny that has so long cramped its energies, and allowed to take its place among the free and progressive peoples of the world. It is the only one of the native races of Western Asia that is capable of restoring productive industry and assured prosperity to these now desolated regions that were the earliest homes of civilization.

James Bryce

ARMENIA'S LOVE TO SHAKESPEARE

BY ZABELLE C. BOYAJIAN

A great festival was held on the tercentenary of Shakespeare's death in 1916. Miss Boyajian was one of many authors who paid tribute at that time to the King of the Bards. Her poem was published in the Book of Homage to Shakespeare (London, 1916), edited by Sir Israel Gollancz, a famous Shakespearean scholar, at that time Professor of English Literature at King's College in London, and at Cambridge.

> Great, unknown spirit, living with us still,
> Though three long centuries have marked thy flight;
> Is there a land thy presence doth not fill
> A race to which thou hast not brought delight?
>
> To me Armenia seems thy house, for first,
> Thy visions there enthralled my wondering mind,
> And thy sweet music with my heart conversed—
> Armenia in thy every scene I find.
>
> Through all the gloom of strife and agony
> Thy gentle light, beloved of all, doth shine;
> The nations bring their tribute unto thee,
> To honor thee thy country's foes combine.
>
> What token shall my poor Armenia bring?
> No golden diadem her brow adorns;
> All jeweled with tears, and glistening,
> She lays upon thy shrine her Crown of Thorns.

REPROACHES

BY KHACHATUR KECHARETZI "FRIK"
(Died 1330)

O GOD of righteousness and truth,
Loving to all, and full of ruth;
I have some matter for Thine ear
If Thou wilt but Thy servant hear.

Lo, how the world afflicteth us
With wrongs and torments rancorous;
And Thou dost pardon every one,
But turnest from our woes alone.

Lord, Thou wilt not avenge our wrong
Nor chase the ills that round us throng;
Thou knowest, we are flesh and bone,
We are not statues made from stone!

We are not made of grass or reeds,
That Thou consumest us like weeds;—
As though we were some thorny field
Or brushwood, that the forests yield.

If that ourselves are nothing worth—
If we have wrought no good on earth,
If we are hateful in Thy sight
That Thou shouldst leave us in this plight—

Then blot us out;—be swift and brief,
That Thy pure heart may find relief;
This well may be, by Thy intent,
Great Lord and good, omnipotent.

How long must we in patience wait
And bear unmurmuringly our fate?
Let evil ones be swept away
And those whom Thou dost favour, stay!

A TRIAL OF ORTHODOXY

(Sonnet on Armenia)

BY WILLIAM WATSON

THE clinging children at their mother's knee
  Slain; and the sire and kindred one by one
  Flayed or hewn piecemeal; and things nameless done,
Not to be told: while imperturbably
The nations gaze, where Rhine unto the sea,
  Where Seine and Danube, Thames and Tiber run,
  And where great armies glitter in the sun,
And great Kings rule, and man is boasted free!
  What wonder if yon torn and naked throng
Should doubt a Heaven that seems to wink and nod,
  And having mourned at noontide, "Lord, how long?"
  Should cry, "Where hidest Thou?" at evenfall,
At midnight, "Is He deaf and blind, our God?"
  And ere day dawn, "Is He indeed at all?"

THE EXILE'S SONG

FOLK SONG

BELOVÈD one, for thy sweet sake,
By whirlwinds tossed and swayed I roam;
The stranger's accents round me wake
These burning thoughts that wander home.
No man such longings wild can bear
As in my heart forever rise.
Oh that the wind might waft me there
Where my belovèd's vineyard lies!
Oh that I were the zephyr fleet,
That bends her vines and roses sweet.

For I am piteous and forlorn,
As is the bird that haunts the night;
Who inconsolably doth mourn
Whene'er his rose is from his sight.
O'er earth and ocean, everywhere
I gaze in vain, with weary eyes.
Oh that the wind might waft me there
Where my belovèd's vineyard lies!
Oh that I were the zephyr fleet
That bends her vines and roses sweet.

I would I were yon cloud so light,—
Yon cloudlet driven before the wind.
Or yonder bird with swift-winged flight:
My heart's true way I soon would find!
Oh, I would be the wind so fleet
That bends her vines and roses sweet.

THE APPLE TREE

FOLK SONG

THE door of Heaven open seemed
And in thy house the sunlight gleamed.

As through the garden's willow'd walks I hied
Full many a tree and blossom I espied.
But of all trees, the Apple Tree most fair
And beautiful did unto me appear.
It sobbed and wept. Its leaves said murmuringly:
"I would that God had ne'er created me!
The badge of sin and wickedness I am
E'en at thy feast, O Father Abraham.
   The apple growing on me first
   From Eden came ere it was cursed,
   Alas, alas, I am undone!
   Why fell I to that evil one?"

MY HEART IS TURNED INTO A WAILING CHILD

BY N. KOUCHAK

(Fifteenth Century)

MY heart is turned into a wailing child,
   In vain with sweets I seek to still its cries;
Sweet love, it calls for thee in sobbing wild
   All day and night, with longing and with sighs.
     What solace can I give it?

I showed my eyes the fair ones of this earth
   And tried to please them—but I tried in vain.
Sweet love, for them all those were nothing worth—
   Thee—only thee my heart would have again.
     What solace can I give it?

O NIGHT, BE LONG

BY N. KOUCHAK

O NIGHT, be long—long as an endless year!
Descend, thick darkness, black and full of fear!
   To-night my heart's desire has been fulfilled—
   My love is here at last—a guest concealed!

Dawn, stand behind seven mountains—out of sight,
Lest thou my loved one banish with thy light;
   I would for ever thus in darkness rest
   So I might ever clasp him to my breast.

BLACK EYES

BY AVETIS ISAHAKIAN

(Born 1875)

Do not trust black eyes, but fear them:—
  Gloom they are, and endless night;
Woes and perils lurking near them
  Love not thou their gleaming bright!

In my heart a sea of blood wells,
  Called up by their cruel might,
No calm ever in that flood dwells
  Love not thou their gleaming bright!

YESTERNIGHT I WALKED ABROAD

YESTERNIGHT I walked abroad.
From the clouds sweet dews were falling,
 And my love stood in the road,
All in green, and to me calling.
 To her home she led me straight,
Shut and barred the gate securely;
 Whoso tries to force that gate
Brave I'll reckon him most surely!

 In the garden she did go,
Gathered roses dewed with showers;
 Some she gave her lover, so
He might lay his face in flowers.

 Garments loose and snowy breast,
I slipped in her bosom tender
 And I found a moment's rest,
Clasped within those arms so slender.
Then I raised my hands above—
Grant, O Lord, that I wake never;
On the bosom of my love
May I live and die forever!

What have I from this world gained?
What advantage gathered ever?
For the hunt my falcon trained
I let fly—it went forever!

Ah, my falcon, woe the day!
Tell me, whither art thou flying
I will follow all the way—
Since thou wentest I am dying.

 I am ill, and near my end—
With an apple[1] hasten to me.

---

[1] An apple is the symbol of love.

I shall curse thee if thou send
Strange physicians to undo me.

No physicians strange for me—
All my griefs in thee I centre.
    Come and take my bosom's key,
Open wide the door and enter.
    Once again I say, 'twas not
I that came—'twas thy love brought me.
    In my heart thy love hath got
And its dwelling-place hath wrought me.

When the falcon hunger feels
Then he finds the game and takes it;
    When love thirsts, the lover steals
Kisses from his love and slakes it.
    But thou hold'st me with thy charms;
When I kiss thee thou dost bind me:
    'Twas but now I left thine arms,
And my looks are turned behind me.
    I am ever, for thy love,
Like the sands in summer, burning:
    Looking up to heaven above,
For one little raindrop yearning.

I would kiss thy forehead chaste,
And thine eyes so brightly gleaming;
    Fold mine arms about thy waist—
Thick with all thy garments seeming.

Oft and often have I said
For my love make garments shining:
    Of the sun the facing red,—
Of the moon cut out the lining;
    Pad it with yon storm-cloud dark,
Sewn with sea weed from the islets:
    Stars for clasps must bring their spark—
Stitch me inside for the eyelets!

VAHAGN, KING OF ARMENIA

From the History of Armenia,

By

MOSES OF KHORENE

(Fifth Century)

CONCERNING the birth of this king the legends say—

> "Heaven and earth were in travail,
> And the crimson waters were in travail.
> And in the water, the crimson reed
> Was also in travail.
> From the mouth of the reed issued smoke,
> From the mouth of the reed issued flame.
> And out of the flame sprang the young child.
> His hair was of fire, a beard had he of flame,
> And his eyes were suns."

With our own ears did we hear these words sung to the accompaniment of the harp. They sing, moreover, that he did fight with the dragons, and overcame them; and some say that his valiant deeds were like unto those of Hercules. Others declare that he was a god, and that a great image of him stood in the land of Georgia, where it was worshipped with sacrifices.

HUNTSMAN, THAT ON THE HILLS ABOVE

BY AVETIS ISAHAKIAN

"HUNTSMAN, that on the hills above
  To hunt the deer hast been,
Tell me, I pray thee, if my love—
  My wild deer thou hast seen?

"He sought the hills his grief to quell—
  My darling love, my sun.
He wandered out upon the fell,
  My flower, my only one."

"Maiden, I saw your lover true,
  All girt with red and green.
Upon his breast a rose tree grew
  Where once your kiss had been."

"Huntsman, I pray, who is the bride
  Of my beloved, my sun?
Who tends him, watching by his side,
  My flower, my only one?"

"Maiden, I saw him with his head
  Upon a stone at rest.
And for his love, a bullet red
  Into his heart was pressed.

"The mountain breeze caressingly
  Played with his jet-black hair,
And blossoms wept unceasingly
  Your flower, your lover there."

LIBERTY

BY MIKAEL NALBANDIAN

(1829-1866)

WHEN the God of Liberty
Formed of earth this mortal frame,
Breathed the breath of life in me,
And a spirit I became,

Wrapped within my swaddling bands,
Bound and fettered helplessly, [2]
I stretched forth my infant hands
To embrace sweet Liberty.

All night long, until the dawn,
In my cradle bound I lay;
And my sobbing's ceaseless moan
Drove my mother's sleep away.

As I begged her, weeping loud,
To unbind and set me free;
From that very day I vowed
I would love thee, Liberty!

When upon my parents' ear
First my lisping accents fell,
And their hearts rejoiced to hear
Me my childish wishes tell,

Then the words that first I spoke
Were not "father, mother dear":
"Liberty!" the accents broke
In my infant utterance clear.

---

[2] Armenian babies were tied tightly into their cradles when they are put to sleep.

"Liberty!" The voice of Doom
Echoed to me from above,
"Wilt thou swear until the tomb
Liberty to serve and love?

"Thorny is the path, and dim;
Many trials wait for thee:
Far too small this world for him
Who doth worship Liberty!"

"Liberty!" I made reply,
"O'er my head let thunders burst,
Lightnings flash, and missiles fly—
Foes conspire to do their worst;

"Till I die, or meet my doom,
On the shameful gallows-tree,-
Till the portals of the tomb,
I will shout forth Liberty!"

I BEHELD MY LOVE THIS MORNING

BY SAYAT NOVA

(1712-1795)

I BEHELD my love this morning, in the garden paths she
   strayed,
All brocaded was the ground with prints her golden
   pattens made;
Like the nightingale, I warbled round my rose with wings
   displayed,
And I wept, my reason faltered, while my heart was sore
   dismayed.
Grant, O Lord, that all my foemen to such grief may be
   betrayed!

Love, with these thy whims and humours thou hast
   wrecked and ruined me.
Thou hast drunk of love's own nectar, thy lips speak
   entrancingly.
With those honeyed words how many like me thou hast
   bound to thee!
Take the knife and slay me straightway—pass not by me
   mockingly.
Since I die of love, 'twere better Beauty stabbed and set
   me free.

For I have no love beside thee—I would have thee know it
   well.
Thou for whom e'en death I'd suffer, list to what I have to
   tell.
See thou thwart not thy Creator, all the past do not dispel:
Anger not thy Sayat Nova, for when in thy snare he fell
He was all bereft of reason by thy whims' and humours'
   spell.

THE FOX, THE WOLF, AND THE BEAR

FOLK SONG

THE little fox, the wolf and bear made peace;
Like kinsfolk all, they bade their warfare cease.
The fox they consecrate a hermit now;—
False monk, false hermit, false recluse's vow!

The little fox a sack found in the street
Through which he thrust his head; then shod his feet
With iron shoes, and got a staff, I trow—
False monk, false hermit, false recluse's vow!

The fox has sent the wolf to fetch the bear.
"For him," he said, "I live this life of care;
Yet never hath he sent me aught to eat:—
Sore are my knees with walking, sore my feet!"

At morning dawn forth to the hunt they creep;
A ram they catch, a lambkin and a sheep.
Holy dispenser is the wolf proclaimed—
Unjust dispenser, judge unwisely named!

He gives the sheep as portion to the bear;
The lambkin falls to the poor hermit's share.
"The ram for me," he said, "I'm tired and lamed"—
Unjust dispenser, judge unwisely named!

The bear was wroth, and turned him round about,
And with one blow the wolf's two eyes put out.
"That sheep for me, a bear so great and famed?
Unjust dispenser, judge unwisely named!"

The little fox is sore afraid, and sees
A trap laid ready with a piece of cheese.
"O uncle, see, I've built a convent here,"
He said, "a place of rest, a place of prayer!"

The bear stretched out his paw for the repast,
The trap upon his neck closed hard and fast.
"Help me, my little nephew, for I fear
This is no convent, 'tis no house of prayer!"

The little fox with joy beheld the whole
And sang a mass for his great uncle's soul.
"The wrong thou didst the wolf has brought thee there;
It is a house of rest, a house of prayer!"

O sovereign Justice, much thou pleasest me—
Who wrongs another soon shall cease to be.
And fasting in the trap must lie the bear,—
For 'tis a house of rest, a house of prayer!"

INCENSE

BY ZABELLE ESSAYAN

(Born 1878)

THE incense at the altar slowly burns
Swayed in the silver censer to and fro;
Around the crucifix it coils and turns,
The brows of saints it wreathes with misty glow.

And tremulous petitions, long drawn out,
Beneath the lofty arches faint away;
To weary eyes the candles round about
Heave as they flicker with their pallid ray.

The sacred columns, grey and mouldering,
Support a veil that stirs with voiceless sobs.
Beneath it, like the incense smouldering,
A woman's darkened heart in anguish throbs.

Consumed within the censer now, and burned,
The incense through the boundless ether soars.
What Matter was to Fragrance sweet is turned—
The cleansing fire its purity restores.

Nor shall that woman's smouldering heart be freed,—
Saved from its cold and adamantine shell,—
Till it is melted, tried, and cleansed indeed,
Till the pure flames shall all its dross expel!

THE LITTLE LAKE [3]

BY BEDROS TOURIAN

(1852-1872)

WHY dost thou lie in hushed surprise,
  Thou little lonely mere?
Did some fair woman wistfully
  Gaze in thy mirror clear?

Or are thy waters calm and still
  Admiring the blue sky,
Where shining cloudlets, like thy foam,
  Are drifting softly by?

Sad little lake, let us be friends!
  I too am desolate;
I too would fain, beneath the sky,
  In silence meditate.

As many thoughts are in my mind
  As wavelets o'er thee roam;
As many wounds are in my heart
  As thou hast flakes of foam.

But if heaven's constellations all
  Should drop into thy breast,
Thou still wouldst not be like my soul,—
  A flame-sea without rest.

There, when the air and thou are calm;
  The clouds let fall no showers;

---

[3] This and the other translations by Miss Alice Stone Blackwell are reprinted
from Armenian Poems, by the translator's kind permission.

22

The stars that rise there do not set,
  And fadeless are the flowers.

Thou art my queen, O little lake!
  For e'en when ripples thrill
Thy surface, in thy quivering depths
  Thou hold'st me, trembling, still.

Full many have rejected me:
  "What has he but his lyre?"
"He trembles, and his face is pale;
  His life must soon expire!"

None said, "Poor child, why pines he thus?
  If he beloved should be,
Haply he might not die, but live,
  Live, and grow fair to see."

None sought the boy's sad heart to read,
  Nor in its depths to look.
They would have found it was a fire,
  And not a printed book!

Nay, ashes now! a memory!
  Grow stormy, little mere,
For a despairing man has gazed
  Into thy waters clear!

SPRING

BY HOVHANNES HOVHANNESSIAN

(Born 1869)

NONE await thy smiling rays;
Whither comest thou, O Spring
None are left to sing thy praise—
Vain thy coming now, O Spring!

All the world is wrapped in gloom,
Earth in blood is weltering:
This year brought us blackest doom—
Whither comest thou, O Spring?

No rose for the nightingale,
No flower within park or dale,
Every face with anguish pale—
Whither comest thou, O Spring?

CRADLE SONG

BY RAPHAEL PATKANIAN

(1830-1892)

Mother

SWEET slumber now creeps o'er thee slow,
Sweet breezes rock thee to and fro:
My baby sleeps, so soft and low
With sweetest songs I'll sing oror. [4]

Baby

O Mother dear, thou art unkind
My sleepless eyes so long to bind. [5]
Anon I'll rest, and sleep resigned;—
Release me now, sing not oror.

Mother

Why dost thou shed those tears that flow
Down thy sad cheeks with pearly glow '
Thou'lt break thy heart with sobbing so,—
Whom wilt thou have to sing oror?

Baby

At least my hands and feet unbind—
My tender limbs are all confined;
That gentle sleep my eyes may find,
Then tie me in, and sing oror.

---

[4] Oror--lullaby.

[5] Armenian babies had their eyes bandaged when they are put to sleep, and
they are tied into their cradles.

Mother

That tongue of thine is passing sweet,
Yet with thy yards I cannot mete.
Thou wilt not sleep, but at thy feet
Wouldst have me sit, and sing oror.

Baby

All piteously I raise my prayer,
I sob and cry, thou dost not hear.
Thy sweet voice seems to charm thine ear—
I weep, thou singest still oror.

Mother

Hush, hush, and sleep, my baby dear.
My love shall guard thee, year by year,
Until my rose-tree blossoms fair,
Then 'neath his shade I'll sing oror.

Baby

Thy heart is made of stone, I see.
I wept and wept, all uselessly.
Now I shall sleep, I can't be free,
All night, all night sing me oror!

ARA AND SEMIRAMIS

From the History of Armenia,

by

MOSES OF KHORENE

FOR a few years before the death of Ninus, Ara reigned over Armenia under his Protectorate, and found the same favour in his eyes as his father Aram had done. But that wanton and lustful woman Semiramis, having heard speak for many years of the beauty of Ara, wished to possess him; only she ventured not to do anything openly. But after the death or the escape to Crete of Ninus, as it hath been affirmed unto me, she discovered her passion freely, and sent messengers to Ara the Beautiful with gifts and offerings, with many prayers and promises of riches; begging him to come to her to Nineveh and either wed her and reign over all that Ninus had possessed, or fulfil her desires and return in peace to Armenia, with many gifts.

And when the messengers had been and returned many times and Ara had not consented, Semiramis became very wroth; and she arose and took all the multitude of her hosts and hastened to the land of Armenia, against Ara. But, as she had beforehand declared, it was not so much to kill him and persecute him that she went, as to subdue him and bring him by force to fulfil the desires of her passion. For having been consumed with desire by what she had heard of him, on seeing him she became as one beside herself. She arrived in this turmoil at the plains of Ara, called after him Ararat. And when the battle was about to take place she commanded her generals to devise some means of saving the life of Ara. But in the fighting the army of Ara was beaten, and Ara died, being slain by the warriors of Semiramis. And after the battle the Queen sent out to the battlefield to search for the body of her beloved amongst those who had died. And they found the body of Ara amongst the brave ones that had fallen, and she commanded them to place it in an upper chamber in her castle.

But when the hosts of Armenia arose once more against Queen Semiramis to avenge the death of Ara, she said: "I have commanded the gods to lick his wounds, and he shall live again." At the same time she thought to bring Ara back to life by witchcraft and charms, for she was maddened by the intensity of her desires. But when the body began to decay, she commanded them to cast it into a deep pit, and to cover it. And having dressed up one of her men in secret, she sent forth the fame of him thus: "The gods have licked Ara and have brought him back to life again, thus fulfilling our prayers and our pleasure. Therefore from this time forth shall they be the more glorified and worshipped by us, for that they are the givers of joy and the fulfillers of desire." She also erected a new statue in honor of the gods and worshipped it with many sacrifices, showing unto all as if the gods had brought Ara back to life again. And having caused this report to be spread over all the land of Armenia and satisfied the people she put an end to the fighting. And she took the son of Ara whom his beloved wife Nouvart had borne unto him and who was but twelve years old at the time of his father's death. And she called his name Ara in memory of her love for Ara the Beautiful, and appointed him ruler over the land of Armenia, trusting him in all things.

LAMENT OVER THE HEROES FALLEN IN THE BATTLE OF AVARAYR

BY KAREKIN SRVANSTIAN

(1840-1892)

IF Goghtan's bards no longer crown
   Armenia's heroes with their lays,
Let deathless souls from Heaven come down,
   Our valiant ones to praise!

Ye shining angel hosts, descend:
   On Ararat's white summit pause;
Let God Himself the heavens rend,
   To come and judge our cause.

Fly, clouds, from Shavarshan away,
   Pour not on it your gentle rain:—
'Tis drenched with streams of blood to-day
   Shed by our brave ones slain.

Henceforth the rose and asphodel
   No more shall on our plains appear;
But in the land where Vartan fell
   Shall Faith her blossoms rear.

Fit monument to Vartan's name,
   Mount Ararat soars to the sky.
And Cross-crowned convents tell his fame,
   And churches vast and high.

Thy record too shall ever stand,
   O Eghishé, for where they fell,
Thou forthwith camest, pen in hand,
   Their faith and death to tell.

Bright sun, pierce with thy rays the gloom,
   Where Khaghdik's crags thy light repel,

There lies our brave Hmayag's tomb,—
   There, where he martyred fell.

And, moon, thy sleepless vigil keep
   O'er our Armenian martyrs' bones;
With the soft dews of Maytime steep
   Their nameless funeral stones.

Armenia's Stork, our summer guest,
   And all ye hawks and eagles, come,
Watch o'er this land—'tis our bequest—
   We leave to you our home.

About the ashes hover still,
   Your nests among the ruins make;
And, swallows, come and go until
   Spring for Armenia break!

THE SONG OF THE STORK

FOLK SONG

STORK, I welcome thy return.
Thou stork, I welcome thy return.
Thy coming is the sign of spring,
And thou dost joy and gladness bring.

Stork, upon our roof descend.
Thou stork, upon our roof descend.
Upon our ash-tree build thy nest,
Our dear one, and our honored guest.

Stork, I would complain to thee:—
Yes, stork, I would complain to thee.
A thousand sorrows I would tell,
The griefs that in my bosom dwell.

Stork, when thou our house didst leave,
When last our ash-tree thou didst leave,
Cold, blasting winds the heavens filled,
And all our smiling flowers were killed.

Clouds obscured the brilliant sky;
Dark clouds obscured the brilliant sky.
Up there in flakes they broke the snow,
And Winter killed the flowers below.

From the mountain of Varag,
From that great hill they call Varag,
The snow did all the earth enfold:—
In our green meadow it was cold.

In our garden all was white.
Our little garden all was white.
Our tender rose-trees, fresh and green,
All died of Winter's frost-bite keen.

31

YE MOUNTAIN BLUEBELLS

BY AVETIS ISAHAKIAN

YE mountain bluebells, weep with me,
   And flowers in colored crowds;
Weep, nightingale, on yonder tree,
   Cool winds dropped from the clouds.

All dark around the earth and sky,
   All lonely here I mourn.
My love is gone,—light of my eye;
   I sob and weep forlorn.

Alas, no more he cares for me—
   He left me unconsoled;
He pierced my heart, then cruelly
   Left me in pain untold.

Ye mountain bluebells, weep with me,
   And flowers in colored crowds;
Weep, nightingale, on yonder tree,—
   Cool winds dropped from the clouds.

THE SUN WENT DOWN

BY AVETIS ISAHAKIAN

THE sun went down behind the hill,
 No light was on the lea,
The fowls and birds slept calm and still,
 But sleep came not to me.

The moon peeped in beneath the eaves,
 The Balance rose on high,
The fresh night-wind that stirred the leaves
 Spoke to the starry sky.

Ah, gentle winds and stars of light,
 Where is my love to-night?
Ye painted eyes of heaven so bright,—
 Saw you my love to-night?

Day dawned,—unbolted was our door:—
 The snowflakes whirled like foam,
'Tis cloud and storm, the wild winds roar
 Why comes my love not home?

BIRTHDAY SONG

BY NAHABED KOUCHAK

ON the morning of thy birth
    We were glad but thou wert wailing,
See that when thou leav'st the earth
    Thou art glad and we bewailing.

Let me speak unto thy heart,—
    List if thou hast understanding;
Keep thyself from fools apart,
    All their flatteries withstanding.

For the fool, like fire and heat,
    Scorcheth everything, and burneth;
But the wise, like water sweet,
    Deserts into gardens turneth.

MORNING

BY HAROUTUNE TOUMANIAN

DAY dawned. Bright tongues of scarlet flame
   Shot up into the sky,
The livid heav'ns blushed, and became
   A sea of crimson dye.

The sun his fiery beams unrolled
   Like strands of colored thread;
Embroidered all the clouds with gold,
   And blue, and green, and red.

Then o'er the mountain, full in view,
   Nature's great Monarch rose:
And from his tent of Royal blue
   Hurled darts upon his foes.

Eternal foe of Gloom and Night,
   On high he raised his arm;
His shield of gold, all shining bright,
   Sheltered the world from harm.

THE FOUNDING OF VAN

BY MOSES OF KHORENE

AND after these things Semiramis, having remained in the plain called Ararat after Ara, went into the hill country towards the south. For it was summer time and she wished to disport herself in the valleys and the flowery plains. And seeing the beauty of the land and the purity of the air, the clearness of the fountains and the murmuring of the gliding rivers, she said, "It is needful that we build for ourselves a city and palaces in this balmy clime and beautiful country, by the side of these pure waters; so that we may spend the fourth part of the year, which is the summer season, with enjoyment in the land of Armenia; and the three cool seasons of the year we will spend in Nineveh."

And passing over many places she came to the eastern shore of the salt lake. And on the shore of the lake she saw a long hill lying towards the setting sun. And south of the hill was a wide valley like unto a plain, which came down from the eastern flank of the hill unto the shore of the lake, spacious and of goodly shape. And the rills of sweet water descending from the mountains ran down the ravines, and meeting around the spurs of the hills they hastened to join the river. And there were not a few buildings erected in the valley on the right and left banks of the waters. And she selected a small hill on the eastern side. After gazing thence for a while that evil and hard-hearted woman Semiramis commanded that twelve thousand unskilled workmen and six thousand of her chosen men skilled in all manner of wood, stone, copper, and iron work should be brought from Assyria and all other lands to the desired place. And it was done according to her command. And immediately a great multitude of diverse workmen were brought, and of wise and gifted workers in all the arts. And she commanded first to make the dyke of the river, of boulders and great rocks cemented together with clay, of great width and height; the which it is said remains firm until this day, so that in the clefts of these dykes pirates and exiles do fortify themselves as in the caves of the mountains, none being able to wrench even one stone from the dyke. And when one looked upon the cement it appeared like a torrent of fat. Thus having taken the dyke round over much ground she brought it unto the intended site of the city. There she commanded the multitude of the workers to be divided into diverse sections, placing over each section a chosen master of the arts. And under such oppression did she keep them that after a few years the wondrous rampart with its gates of wrought copper was completed. And she made beautiful buildings in the city, and palaces of different stones decorated with colors, two stories and three stories high. For each one she did build summer-houses, separating the various quarters of the town from each other by beautiful streets. She built also wondrous baths in the midst of the city for the use of the people, and divided the water passing through the town into two parts, one for watering the fragrant orchards and flower-gardens, and the other for the drinking water of the city and its surroundings. On the east, north, and south of the city she built pleasure houses, and planted orchards with leafy trees that bore diverse kinds of fruit and foliage; she also planted many vines. The whole city she surrounded with stately ramparts, and caused great multitudes to dwell therein.

But concerning the far end of the city, and the miraculous works that were done there, it surpassed the power of a man to tell; neither can they be understood by man. For there, surrounded by fortifications, she did construct the Royal Palace, in great mystery. For the entrances were hard, and the passages leading out of it like those of hell. Concerning the manner of its making we have never read a true description, neither do we propose to weave it into our history; but we only say that of all royal works it is, as we have heard, esteemed the first and greatest. And on the west side of the rock—whereon no man can now make any impression, even with iron—in this adamantine substance she constructed many temples, bed-chambers, and treasure-houses; and great trenches, so that none knoweth for what manner of things she made these marvelous preparations. And smoothing the face of the rock as one would smooth wax with a pen, she wrote many inscriptions thereon; so that even to look at it caused a man to be amazed.

I HAVE A WORD I FAIN WOULD SAY

BY SAYAT NOVA

I HAVE a word I fain would say—list patiently, Light of
    my Eyes;
A ceaseless longing fills my heart thy face to see, Light of
    my Eyes.
How have I sinned that thou shouldst thus offended be,
    Light of my Eyes
The world is sated with the world,—I starve for thee, Light
    of my Eyes.

A sea of blood is in my heart, and tears forever fill my
    eyes;
No salve can heal my wound, the cure in my beloved's
    presence lies.
All sick of love I lay, and watched her pathway with my
    longing eyes;
When I was dead she came; 'twas but the layer-out who
    heard her sighs.

Fair springtime now is fully here, the meadows gay with
    leaf and flower;
The hill-sides strewn with violets, the nightingale sent to
    the bower.
But why cannot his voice be heard id O thorn-tree, whence
    thy cruel power?
Thy branches pierced . his heart; the rose was mourning
    left within her tower.

The scarlet poppy thought to tempt and lure the
    wandering nightingale,
When he was dreaming of the rose tied round with wisps
    of basil pale.
None pitied him—the rose was plucked by those who first
    came to the vale.
Alas, poor nightingale, the hedge has caught and pierced
    thy body frail!

God knows my life I count but nought; for thee I'd give it
      joyfully.
Come, let us taste of love's delights, let him that listeth
      envious be.
No wish of thine shall be refused, so but thy face I radiant
      see.
If immortality thou'dst have, my love shall e'en bring that
      to thee.

And if I had a thousand woes no murmur from my lips
      would rise:
Thou art my Ruler, none beside; no sovereign own I
      otherwise.
Sayat Nova says, "Heartless one, death is not death for
      him who dies
So thou but mourn him with thy locks spread over him,
      Light of my Eyes."

THE SONG OF THE PARTRIDGE

FOLK SONG

THE sun has touched the mountain's crest,
The partridge rises from her nest;
And down the hillside tripping fast,
Greets all the flowers as she goes past.

I breakfast on my roof at morn
When to my ear her voice is borne—
When swinging from the mountain side,
She chirps her song in all her pride.

Thy nest is dewed with summer showers;
Basil, narcissus, lotus flowers,
Enamel it, and breathe to thee
Perfumes of immortality.

Soft feathers all thy body deck,
Small is thy beak, and long thy neck.
Thy wings are worked with colors rare,
The dove is not so sweet and fair.

The little partridge flies aloft
Upon the branch, and warbles soft;
He cheers the world, and heals the smart
When seas of blood well in the heart.

THE LILY OF SHAVARSHAN

BY LEO ALISHAN

(1820—1901)

ARMENIAN maidens, come and view
In Shavarshan a lily new!

The radiant type of maidenhood,
  Crown of Armenia's pride!
From the fair brow beneath her veil
  The wind-stirred curls float wide
With little steps, like turtle dove,
  She walks the dew-bright plain;
Her lips drop honey, and her eyes
  Effulgent glances rain.

The beauty of Armenia,
  A sun-like mirror clear,
Our Northern star is bright Santoukhd,
  The king's fair daughter dear.
She has come forth, the graceful bride
  On whom the East and West
Desire to look, while fires of love
  Consume the gazer's breast.

Less fair the bright and morning star,
  'Mid cloudlets small and fine;
Less fair the fruit whose rosy tints
  'Mid apple leaves outshine;
Araxes' hyacinthine flower
  That chains of dew doth wear,
All are less beautiful than she,
  With gracious mien and air.

At sight of her, the snowy peaks
  Melt and are flushed with rose;
Trees, flowers bud forth; the nightingales
  All sing where'er she goes.

41

The bell-flowers open myriad eyes
    When she comes through the bowers;
Beneath her breath, the vales and hills
    Alike are clad in flowers.

Before her have been bent to earth
    Foreheads with diadems;
The valley has become a hill
    Of scattered gold and gems.
Where passes by with humble grace
    Armenia's virgin sweet,
Fine sands of pearls come longingly
    To spread beneath her feet.

Full many a monarch's valiant son
    Has left his palace home
In Persia or Albania,
    In India or in Rome.
Admiringly they gaze on her,
    Exclaiming, "Happy he
Who wins the fair Armenian maid
    His bride beloved to be!"

But palace worthy of Santoukhd
    The earth can nowhere show,
And for the arches of her brows
    This world is all too low

The Sky says, "Let her on my throne
    Reign queen o'er every land."
The Ocean says, "My purple waves
    Shall bow to her command."

There is One greater than the earth,
    More wide than sea-waves run,
Higher and vaster than the heavens,
    And brighter than the sun.
There is a formidable King
    Whose power no bound has known;
The royal maid Santoukhd shall be

For Him, and Him alone.
Her halls of light are all prepared,
    And for a footstool meet
The azure sky adorned with stars
    Awaits her dove-like feet.

.   .   .   .   .   .

The sharp sword glitters in the air,
    And swift the red blood flows;
Santoukhd, who was a lily fair,
    Falls to the earth, a rose.
The sword flashed once, and aspects three
    Were in Santoukhd descried;
Her heart dropped blood, and roses red
    Sprang up on every side;
Her eyes were violet chalices,
Sweet e'en while they expire;
    Her face, like lilies half unclosed,
But on her lips what fire!

The heaven and earth shine white and red;
    Come forth and gather, maids,

The rose and lily joined in one,
    This peerless flower that fades!
Lay in the tomb that youthful corpse,
    With Thaddeus, good and brave.
Sweet maiden of Armenia,
    Her sweet soil be thy grave!
Armenian maids, a lily new
Is brought to Shavarshan for you!

Translated by Alice Stone Blackwell.

Santoukhd was martyred by the order of her father, King Sanadroug, for
becoming a Christian.

43

CRADLE SONG

BY RAPHAEL PATKANIAN

NIGHTINGALE, oh, leave our garden,
Where soft dews the blossoms steep;
With thy litanies melodious
Come and sing my son to sleep!
Nay, he sleeps not for thy chanting,
And his weeping hath not ceased.
Come not, nightingale! My darling
Does not wish to be a priest.

O thou thievish, clever jackdaw,
That in coin findest thy joy,
With thy tales of gold and profit
Come and soothe my wailing boy!
Nay, thy chatter does not lull him,
And his crying is not stayed.
Come not, jackdaw! for my darling
Will not choose the merchant's trade.

Wild dove, leave the fields and pastures
Where thou grievest all day long;
Come and bring my boy sweet slumber
With thy melancholy song!
Still he weeps. Nay, come not hither,
Plaintive songster, for I see
That he loves not lamentations,
And no mourner will he be.

Leave thy chase, brave-hearted falcon!
Haply he thy song would hear.
And the boy lay hushed, and slumbered,
With the war-notes in his ear.

Translated by Alice Stone Blackwell.

THE WIND IS HOWLING THROUGH THE WINTER NIGHT

BY AVETIS ISAHAKIAN

THE wind is howling through the winter night,
Like to a pack of angry wolves that cry.
My hapless willows bend before its might;
Their broken branches in the garden lie.

Alas, my heart, thy love since childhood's days
Hath wept; thy dream was understood by none.
Seek not in vain a friend to know thy ways—
The soul is born eternally alone.

Thou from thy hopeless heart that love shalt cast—
That child of earth, false, illegitimate:
Shalt fling it to the night and wintry blast—
Out in the storm—there let it find its fate.

There motherless and orphaned let it weep,
And let the wind its sobbings onward bear
Unto some desert place, or stormy deep—
But not where human soul its voice may hear.

The wind is howling in its agony
All through this snow-bound night, with piercing cry;
Alas, beneath the broken willow tree
My shattered love lies dying—let it die.

THE ARMENIAN POET'S PRAYER

BY ALEXANDER DZADOURIAN

(Born 1870)

O GOD, 'tis not for laurel wreaths I pray,
For pompous funeral or jubilee;
Nor yet for fame beyond my life's decay—
All these my country will accord to me.

One favor, Lord of Heaven, I implore—
One that my land to me will never give:
Grant me a crust of bread, or else such store
Of grace that I on air may learn to live!

THE CHRAGAN PALACE

BY THOMAS TERZYAN

(1842-1909)

HAVE you ever seen that wondrous building,
    Whose white shadows in the blue wave sleep?
There Carrara sent vast mounds of marble,
    And Propontis, beauty of the deep.

From the tombs of centuries awaking,
    Souls of every clime and every land
Have poured forth their rarest gifts and treasures
    Where those shining halls in glory stand.

Ships that pass before that stately palace,
    Gliding by with open sails agleam,
In its shadow pause and gaze, astonished,
    Thinking it some Oriental dream.

New its form, more wondrous than the Gothic,
    Than the Doric or Ionic fair;
At command of an Armenian genius [6]
    Did the master builder rear it there.

By the windows, rich with twisted scroll-work,
    Rising upward, marble columns shine,
And the sunbeams lose their way there, wandering
    Where a myriad ornaments entwine.

An immortal smile, its bright reflection
    In the water of the blue sea lies,
And it shames Granada's famed Alhambra,
    O'er whose beauty wondering bend the skies.

Oft at midnight, in the pale, faint starlight,
    When its airy outline, clear and fair,

---

[6] The late Hagop Bey Balian.

47

On the far horizon is depicted,
    With its trees and groves around it there,

You can fancy that those stones grow living,
    And, amid the darkness of the night,
Change to lovely songs, to which the spirit,
    Dreaming, listens with a vague delight.

Have you ever seen that wondrous building
    Whose white shadows in the blue wave sleep?
There Carrara sent vast mounds of marble,
    And Propontis, beauty of the deep.

It is not a mass of earthly matter,
    Not a work from clay or marble wrought;
From the mind of an Armenian genius
Stands embodied there a noble thought.

Translated by Alice Stone Blackwell.

THE DREAM

BY SMPAD SHAHAZIZ

(1840-1897)

SOFT and low a voice breathed o'er me,
  Near me did my mother seem;
Flashed a ray of joy before me,
  But, alas, it was a dream!

There the murmuring streamlet flowing
  Scattered radiant pearls around,
Pure and clear, like crystal glowing—
  But it was a dream, unsound.

And my mother's mournful singing
  Took me back to childhood's day,
To my mind her kisses bringing—
  'Twas a dream and passed away!

To her heart she pressed me yearning,
  Wiped her eyes which wet did seem;
And her tears fell on me burning—
  Why should it have been a dream?

THE SORROWS OF ARMENIA

IN many a distant, unknown land,
    My sons belovèd exiled roam,
Servile they kiss the stranger's hand;
    How shall I find and bring them home?

The ages pass, no tidings come;
    My brave ones fall, are lost and gone.
My blood is chilled, my voice is dumb,
    And friend or comfort I have none.

With endless griefs my heart is worn,
    Eternal sorrow is my doom;
Far from my sons, despis'd, forlorn,
    I must descend the darksome tomb.

Thou shepherd wandering o'er the hill,
    Come weep with me my children lost;
Let mournful strains the valleys fill
    For those we loved and valued most.

Fly, crane, Armenia's bird, depart;
    Tell them I die of grief; and tell
How hope is dead within my heart—
    Bear to my sons my last farewell!

ARTASHES AND SATENIK

From the History of Armenia,

by

MOSES OF KHORENE

AT this time the Alans united with all the people of the mountain country, and having taken possession of the half of Georgia, spread themselves in great multitudes over our land. And Artashes collected a mighty host together, and there was war between the two great nations. The Alans retreated somewhat, and crossing over the river Kur they encamped on its northern bank. And when Artashes arrived, he encamped on the southern hank, so that the river was between them. But because the son of the King of the Alans was taken captive by the Armenian hosts and brought to Artashes, the King of the Alans sought peace, promising to give to Artashes whatsoever he should ask. And he swore an eternal peace unto him, so that the sons of the Alans might not be carried away captive into the land of the Armenians. And when Artashes would not consent to give back the youth, his sister came to the river's bank and stood upon a great rock. And by means of the interpreters she spoke to the camp of Artashes, saying:—"O brave Artashes, who hast vanquished the great nation of the Alans, unto thee I speak. Come, hearken unto the bright-eyed daughter of the Alan King, and give back the youth. For it is not the way of heroes to destroy life at the root, nor for the sake of humbling and enslaving a hostage to establish everlasting enmity between two great nations." And on hearing such wise sayings, Artashes went to the bank of the river. And seeing that the maiden was beautiful, and having heard these words of wisdom from her, he desired her. And calling Smpad his chamberlain he told him the wishes of his heart, and commanded that he should obtain the maiden for him, swearing unto the great Alan nation oaths of peace, and promising to send the youth back in safety. And this appeared wise in the eyes of Smpad, and he sent messengers unto the King of the Alans asking him to give the lady Satenik his daughter as wife unto Artashes. And the King of the Mans answered, "From whence shall brave Artashes give thousands upon thousands and tens of thousands upon tens of thousands unto the Alans in return for the maiden?"

Concerning this the poets of that land sing in their songs:—

> "Brave King Artashes
> Mounted his fine black charger,
> And took the red leathern cord
> With the golden ring.
> Like a swift-winged eagle
> He passed over the river,
> And cast the golden ring
> Round the waist of the Alan Princess;
> Causing much pain
> To the tender maiden
> As he bore her swiftly
> Back to his camp."

Which being interpreted meaneth that he was commanded to give much gold, leather, and crimson dye in exchange for the maiden. So also they sing of the wedding:—

> "It rained showers of gold when Artashes became a bridegroom.
> It rained pearls when Satenik became a bride."

For it was the custom of our kings to scatter coins amongst the people when they arrived at the doors of the temple for their wedding, as also for the queens to scatter pearls in their bridechamber.

MY DEATH

BY BEDROS TOUR IAN

WHEN Death's pale angel comes to me,
And smiling sweetly on my head,
Bids all my pains and sorrows fleet,—
Believe not then that I am dead.

When my cold limbs they shroud with care,
And on my brow love's tear-drops shed,
And lay me on my ebon bier,—
Believe not then that I am dead.

And when the tolling bell shall ring
To my black coffin's muted tread
—Death's fiendish laughter, quivering,—
Believe not then that I am dead.

And when the black-robed priests shall sing,
And prayers and incense round me spread,
With faces dark and sorrowing—
Believe not still that I am dead.

When on my tomb they heap the clay,
And leave me in my lonely bed,
And loved ones turn with sobs away—
Then never think that I am dead.

But if my grave neglected lie,
My memory too be gone and fled,
And dear ones pass unheeding by,
Ah, then believe that I am dead!

THE EAGLE'S LOVE

BY SHUSHANIK GOURGHINIAN

(Born 1876)

AN eagle sat upon the fell,—
    He sat and sang alone.
A pretty maid passed in the dell,
    He saw—his heart was won.

"Ah, lovely maid, enchanting maid,
    Alas, thou canst not fly!
Down in the vale thou soon shalt fade,
    And like a floweret die.

"I'd make thee queen, if thou could'st fly,
    Of all my mountains steep;
At night I'd sing thy lullaby,
    And in my wings thou'dst sleep.

"Those eyes are like black night to me,
    That smile like sunshine bright;
And heaven itself would quickly be
    Subdued before thy might.

"Good Lord, canst thou not fly at all?
    Who made thee without wings?
Art thou content down there to crawl?
    With loathsome creeping things?"

Thus on his rock the eagle proud
    Sat singing, then he sailed
O'er hill and valley, and aloud
    The maiden's fate bewailed.

CONCERNING THE ROSE AND THE NIGHTINGALE

BY GRIGORIS OF AGHTAMAR

(Fifteenth Century)

THE Rose was gone. When to the empty tent
The Nightingale returned, his heart was torn.
He filled the night with mourning and lament,
And wandered through the darkness lone and lorn.

"To thee I speak, O Garden, answer me,
Why did'st thou not preserve my precious Rose,
Whose perfume breathed of immortality,
Whose colour made her queen of all that grows?

"May'st thou become a desert parched and dry,
And may the flowers that grow within thee fade;
May thy protecting walls in ruin lie—
By ruthless feet thy soil in waste be laid.

"Ye trees, now cast away your verdant leaves,
And rushing torrents, your swift courses stay.
Reckless I speak, as one who sorely grieves,
For they have taken my sweet love away.

"My Rose is gone and I am desolate.
Light of my eyes was she, now darkness reigns.
Both day and night I weep disconsolate.
My reason leaves me, and my spirit wanes.

"Was it the gardener took her away
And grieved my soul If never more again
I should behold her face, what shall I say?
Instead of joy, I'll sing of grief and pain.

"Or else I fear the mighty wind arose,
And blasted with its strength her petals frail;

Or did the scorching sunbeams burn my Rose
Within her leaves, and turn her beauty pale? . . .

"I think perhaps the flowers were wroth with me
And hid her from my sight; I'll go to them.
Or else the clouds in cruel enmity
Sent hailstones down that broke her from the stem!"

Then all the flowers together made reply,
"We have no tidings of the Rose at all,
She left us suddenly, we know not why.
We have no tidings of the Rose at all."

The Nightingale then rose into the air,
"I'll ask the birds in friendly wise," he said,
"If they can tell me why she went, and where;
If not, a sea of tears my eyes shall shed.

"Birds, do you know what came to pass to-day?
The lovely Rose was stolen from her home.
Know you perchance who carried her away?
Have you seen aught, or heard where she doth roam?"

They said, "The Lord Creator knoweth all;
No secrets of the heart from Him are hid.
On Him as witness reverently we call
We have not seen or touched her—God forbid!"

The Nightingale then sadly made reply,
"What will become of me? From night to morn
I have no rest, and I shall surely die,
Parted from her, with ceaseless longings worn.

"If in her stead the world to me were given
I would esteem it but a paltry thing;
If choirs of minstrels sang the songs of heaven,
To me their songs as discords harsh would ring.

"Oh, in what corner have they buried thee?
How shall I e'er forget thy tenderness?

56

My heart and soul are wounded grievously,
All flowers are dead—this place a wilderness.

"The Psalmist's words are now fulfilled in me;
Mournful I go, and like a pelican
About the wilderness roam hopelessly,
Or like an owl the sandy desert scan."

The gardener then with soothing words drew near,
"Weep not, she will return, O Nightingale.
The Violet, her forerunner, is here,
And brings thee messages and words of hail."

Then he rejoiced and blessed the gardener,
"May'st thou in peace upon this earth abide,
Thy garden flourish with its bright allure,
Its circling walls renew their former pride.

"May all thy plants grow verdant once again,
And gently sway about upon the breeze,
May they receive fresh brightness from the rain,
And waft sweet perfume human hearts to please!"

Then did the Nightingale write a letter unto the Rose who
collected all the Flowers and caused it to be read in their
presence.

They took the letter to the Rose's Court,
Where Hazrevart, her minister austere,
Stood on his feet with stately mien and port
And read it out for all the flowers to hear:—

"I greet thee, O beloved of my heart,
And fain would hear concerning this thy rape.
I trust through God's protecting care thou art
Perfect in health, as faultless in thy shape.

"For which with outstretched hands I ever pray,
And beg that length of days be granted thee;

All flowers bend to thee and homage pay,
Thou rulest them in all thy majesty.

"Thy hue is beautiful, thy perfume sweet,
Each morn thou shinest brighter than the sun.
Happy the day when thee once more I meet,—
For thou art full of grace, my spotless one.

"Apart from thee, in humble reverence,
I worship thee, and pray for thy return.
I have no sleep at night for this suspense,
Now Spring is here I ever weep and mourn.

"The icy winter passed—I lived it through,
Still suffering many things because of thee;
They mocked at me, and said thou wast not true—
My Rose had no more love or care for me."

Then sent the Rose unto the Nightingale,
And said: "Behold, I send him many flowers.
And they shall cover mountain, hill, and dale,
My Nightingale shall dwell within those bowers.

"I cannot there return immediately;
A little he must wait, in patient wise:
But if his love is perfectly with me,
Tell him to look for it in Paradise."

The Nightingale rejoiced on hearing this
And said: "The beauteous Rose shall then return!
What tidings wonderful of untold bliss!
For all the world her ransom could not earn."

And when the sun into the Ram had passed,
The thunder rolled, the storm-clouds broke in showers;
Myriads of blossoms o'er the earth were cast:—
He sought the Rose—she was not of those flowers.

Until one morn he saw her foliage green,
Lovely and fresh as it had been before:

The Rose was hidden in a silken screen
And every flower worshipped her once more.

The Nightingale beheld and said: "Thank Heaven!
Blessing and praise from every mouth be breathed;
To Heaven's King be endless glory given—
For in her bud I saw the Rose ensheathed!"

.   .   .   .

Foolish Aghtamartzi, beware this bane,
For this world's love is ever linked with thorn;
A little while 'tis gladness, then 'tis pain
What boots the joy which needs must make us mourn?

THE ARRIVAL OF THE CRUSADERS

BY SAINT NERSES SHNORHALI

(1102-1173)

ONCE more God hither moves their course;
With countless infantry and horse,
As swell the waves towards the strand,
Fierce and tempestuous, they land.
Like sands that by the ocean lie,
Or like the stars that strew the sky,
They fill the earth where'er they go
And whiten it as wool or snow.
Their voice is like the northern wind,
Driving the storm-cloud from behind.
They clear the land from end to end,
The unbelievers forth they send,
Redeeming from such hopeless plight
All Christians held within their might.
Now in the churches cold and dark,
Once more shall burn the taper's spark;
And you, my sons, late forced to flee
To distant lands, afar from me,
Shall now return in chariots fair
Drawn by brave steeds with trappings rare.
And I shall lift mine eyes above
Beholding near me those I love.
My arms about you I shall fold,
Rejoicing with a joy untold;
And my black robes aside will lay
To dress in greens and crimsons gay.

LIKE AN OCEAN IS THIS WORLD

BY HOVHANNES ERZINGATZI

(Born 1260)

LIKE an ocean is this world;
None undrenched may cross that ocean.
My ship too its sails unfurled,
Ere I knew it was in motion.

Now we draw towards the land,
And I fear the sea-board yonder:—
Lest the rocks upon the strand
Break and tear our planks asunder.

I will pray God that He raise
From the shore a breeze to meet us,
To disperse this gloomy haze,
That a happy land may greet us.

THE ROCK

BY HOVHANNES HOVHANNESSIAN

ABOVE the waters, like a hoary giant,
The rock stands up, majestic and defiant.
The little waves, as to and fro they move,
Greet him with kisses and with looks of love.

The wavelets of the river laugh and dance,
As in their arms the mirrored sunbeams glance;
And with their smiles of winning, child-like grace,
They woo the rock, and murmur in his face:

"O Aged-One, why art thou never glad?
The lines that seam thy countenance are sad.
The world is ever changing; thou alone
Art still the same with thy dark face of stone.

"Free children of the mountains ever free,
We bring rich gifts of jewels unto thee;
Scent thee with perfumes of the mountain rose—
Heaven's daughter fair, that on our margin grows.

"Sweet strains of gentle melody we breathe,
And call the fishes from our depths beneath;
And gilded with the spring-tide's golden rays,
We make thee on our merry revels gaze.

"And songs of love we warble in thine ear,
From morning dawn until the stars appear:—
We fondle thee, and on thine aged breast
Our passions lull, and bid them sink to rest."

The wavelets hasten, moving to and fro,
The rock still sorrows o'er his ancient woe;
The wavelets play, and laughing onward press—
The rock remains, gloomy and motionless.

THE CRANE

BY HOVHANNES TOUMANIAN

(Born 1869)

THE Crane has lost his way across the heaven,
From yonder stormy cloud I hear him cry,
A traveller o'er an unknown pathway driven,
In a cold world unheeded he doth fly.

Ah, whither leads this pathway long and dark,
My God, where ends it, thus with fears obsessed?
When shall night end this day's last glimmering spark?
Where shall my weary feet to-night find rest?

Farewell, belovèd bird, where'er thou roam
Spring shall return and bring thee back once more,
With thy sweet mate and young ones, to thy home—
Thy last year's nest upon the sycamore.

But I am exiled from my ruined nest,
And roam with faltering steps from hill to hill,
Like to the fowls of heaven in my unrest
Envying the boulders motionless and still.

Each boulder unassailed stands in its place,
But I from mine must wander tempest tossed—
And every bird its homeward way can trace,
But I must roam in darkness, lone and lost.

Ah, whither leads this pathway long and dark,
My God, where ends it, thus with fears obsessed?
When shall night end this day's last glimmering spark?
Where shall my weary feet to-night find rest?

THE HAWK AND THE DOVE

FOLK SONG

THE Hawk said to the Dove, "My dear,
Why dost thou shed tear after tear,
That go to swell the streamlet clear?"
The Dove said to the Hawk, "I fear
That spring is gone and autumn's here;
The rills have ceased their glad career,
The leaves and flowers are dead and sere,
The partridges no more we hear;
So I shall weep in my despair,
And from my eyes shed many a tear:—
How shall I find my babies' fare?"
He said, "Weep not this autumn drear,
For spring will come another year,
And sunshine bring the world its cheer,
And Hope shall for the poor appear.
Upon my pinions thee I'll bear
Where those tall trees their summit rear,
And high upon those mountains bare
I'll build a nest with tender care,
I'll make for thee a dwelling there,—
A hearth laid in that rocky lair,
With chimney open to the air;
The smoke shall to the clouds repair—
And to the South Wind fly our care!"
Autumn gave place to springtime fair,

The rills were loosed on their career
And went to swell the streamlet clear,
Like blood-drops from the boulders bare.
Bright yellow flowers the hills did wear,
And violets, with perfume rare,
And flowers of countless colors fair;
And birds with music filled the air,
And bleating lambs called everywhere
To God for all His love and care.

ARTAVASD

From the History of Armenia

by

MOSES OF KHORENE

AFTER the death of Artashes his son Artavazd reigned, and he drove all his brothers and sisters to the lands of Aghyovd and Arberan, that they might not live in Ararat, on the territory of the King. And when he had reigned but a little while, as he was riding over the bridge of Artashat to hunt deer and wild asses on the banks of the Ghin, he was seized by some visionary terror and lost his reason. And urging his horse down a steep bank he fell into a chasm, wherein he sank and disappeared.

The singers of Ghogtan tell concerning him, that when his father was dying many people killed themselves according to the customs of the heathen; and they say that Artavazd was wroth, and said unto his father:

> "Now that thou art gone
> And hast taken with thee the whole land,
> How shall I reign over the ruins?"

Therefore Artashes cursed him, and said:

> "When thou ridest forth to hunt
> Over the free heights of Ararat,
> The Strong Ones shall have thee,
> And shall take thee up
> On to the free heights of Ararat.
> There shalt thou abide,
> And never more see the light."

Old women also tell of him how that he is confined in a cavern and bound with iron chains. And his two dogs do daily try to gnaw through the chains to set him free, that he may come and put an end to the world; but at the sound of the hammers

65

striking on the anvil, the chains are strengthened. So also even in our own times many blacksmiths do keep up the tradition and strike the anvil three or four times on a Monday, to strengthen, as they say, the chains of Artavazd. But the truth concerning him is as we have declared above.

Others say that at his birth the women of the house of Ahasuerus did try to bewitch him, and therefore Artashes tormented them much; and these same singers say also that the Children of the Dragons stole the infant Artavazd and put a devil in his place. But unto us it seemeth that being full of wickedness from his very birth, so also did he end.

CHARM VERSES 7

FOLK SONGS

SNOWLESS hang the clouds to-night,
Through the darkness comes no light;
    While my lover, far away,
Line or letter will not write.

*   *   *

Snowless hang the clouds to-night,
Through the darkness comes no light;
    On this lonely pillow now,
Never more shall sleep alight.

*   *   *

Like a star whose brightness grows
On the earth my beauty shows;
    Thou shalt long for yet, and seek
My dark eyes and arching brows.

*   *   *

I beheld a dream last night,
Saw these haystacks all alight;—
    They have borne thy love away,—
Wilt not come and for her fight?

*   *   *

---

[7] A great number of these little poems exist. They are traditional, and are used for fortune-telling. On the Eve of Ascension Day all those who wish to have their fortunes told place some little trinket into a bowl containing seven different kinds of flowers and water from seven springs. The bowl is left open to the stars until dawn, when the party assemble and select a child who cannot tell where the sun rises to take the trinkets out as the verses are repeated. The owner of the token takes the verse preceding its being brought out as his or her fortune.

Soft winds move beneath the trees
And thy locks wave in the breeze.
    Whilst thou roamest hill and field
Sleep my eyelids ever flees.

Eden's smile my vineyard wore,
Flowers bloomed, a goodly store;
    Handsome youth and ugly maid—
This was never seen before!

        *   *   *

For the mountain air I'd die,
For his form so fair I'd die,
    Now he's far off, for the eyes
That have seen him there I'd die.

        *   *   *

'Tis a moonlight night to-night,
Eyes so black and cheeks so bright.
    Give me but the one I love—
Peace to you then, and good-night!

        *   *   *

On my finger is a ring,
Crimson rubies, glistening.
    He that parts me from my love,—
Satan to his soul shall cling.

        *   *   *

Long and lone this night to me
Passing slow and wearily;
    Passing full of sighs and tears—
Love, what doth it bring to thee?

        *   *   *

Round the moon a halo grew,
In its depths the storm-cloud drew;
    Go and ask them who it was
Turned from me my lover true.

      *   *   *

Dainty is the frock I wear,
Bright the gauze upon my hair:
    Since my love is coy with me,
I'll be coy, and will not care!

THE TEARS OF ARAXES

BY RAPHAEL PATKANIAN

I WALK by Mother Arax
    With faltering steps and slow,
And memories of past ages
    Seek in the waters' flow.

But they run dark and turbid,
    And beat upon the shore
In grief and bitter sorrow,
    Lamenting evermore.

"Araxes! with the fishes
    Why dost not dance in glee?
The sea is still far distant,
    Yet thou art sad, like me.

"From thy proud eyes, O Mother,
    Why do the tears downpour?
Why dost thou haste so swiftly
    Past thy familiar shore?

"Make not thy current turbid;
    Flow calm and joyously.
Thy youth is short, fair river;
    Thou soon wilt reach the sea.

"Let sweet rose-hedges brighten
    Thy hospitable shore,
And nightingales among them
    Till morn their music pour.

"Let ever-verdant willows
    Lave in thy waves their feet,
And with their bending branches
    Refresh the noonday heat.

"Let shepherds on thy margin
    Walk singing, without fear;
Let lambs and kids seek freely
    Thy waters cool and clear."

Araxes swelled her current,
    Tossed high her foaming tide,
And in a voice of thunder
    Thus from her depths replied:—

"Rash, thoughtless youth, why com'st thou
    My age-long sleep to break,
And memories of my myriad griefs
    Within my breast to wake?

"When hast thou seen a widow,
    After her true-love died,
From head to foot resplendent
    With ornaments of pride?

"For whom should I adorn me?
    Whose eyes shall I delight?
The stranger hordes that tread my banks
    Are hateful in my sight.

"My kindred stream, impetuous Kur,
    Is widowed, like to me,
But bows beneath the tyrant's yoke,
    And wears it slavishly.

"But I, who am Armenian,
    My own Armenians know;
I want no stranger bridegroom;
    A widowed stream I flow.

"Once I, too, moved in splendor,
    Adorned as is a bride
With myriad precious jewels,
    My smiling banks beside.

71

"My waves were pure and limpid,
    And curled in rippling play;
The morning star within them
    Was mirrored till the day.

"What from that time remaineth?
    All, all has passed away.
Which of my prosperous cities
    Stands near my waves to-day?

"Mount Ararat doth pour me,
    As with a mother's care,
From out her sacred bosom
    Pure water, cool and fair.

"Shall I her holy bounty
    To hated aliens fling?
Shall strangers' fields be watered
    From good Saint Jacob's spring?

"For filthy Turk or Persian
    Shall I my waters pour,
That they may heathen rites perform
    Upon my very shore,

"While my own sons, defenseless,
    Are exiled from their home,
And, faint with thirst and hunger,
    In distant countries roam?

"My own Armenian nation
    Is banished far away;
A godless, barbarous people
    Dwells on my banks to-day.

"Shall I my hospitable shores
    Adorn in festive guise
For them, or gladden with fair looks
    Their wild and evil eyes?

"Still, while my sons are exiled,
    Shall I be sad, as now.
This is my heart's deep utterance,
    My true and holy vow."

No more spake Mother Arax;
    She foamed up mightily,
And, coiling like a serpent,
    Wound sorrowing toward the sea.

THE EVE OF ASCENSION DAY [8]

BY DERENIK DEMIRJIAN

NIGHT with her ebon hair and starry crown
  Upon the hills came down.
Her loosened tresses floated all unbound
  And veiled her form around.

The fountain murmured like an endless tale
  On her entrancing lips; and it would seem
As if God spake within the silent vale,
  And sleeping Earth were listening, in a dream.

Like blackened clouds, in Jorokh's stream arise
  Those rocks that through her savage waters pierce;
Like dragons twain, they glare with threatening eyes,
  Facing each other, arrogant and fierce.

Wild Jorokh through that fearsome valley flows—
  Flows like a caravan that onward sweeps;
First roaring loud, then hushed into repose,
  Groping its way through darkness, on it creeps.

The sounds of Earth are melted into rest,
  While strikes the hour of expectation deep;
Earth's waters heave, against each other pressed,
  And breathless listening, all their vigils keep.

Decked out like lovely brides stand all the flowers;
  With nuptial joy the forests trembling wait:
Until Heaven's blessing fall in sacred showers,
  And whispering softly, each may clasp its mate.

---

[8] The Eve of Ascension Day is the time when betrothals are arranged and destinies decided.

"THY VOICE IS SWEET"

BY SAYAT NOVA

THY voice is soft, thy speech all sweetness flows;
May he protect who hath thy heart, my love!
Thy waist is the gazelle's, thy hue the rose,
Brocade from Franguistan thou art, my love!

If I compare thee to brocade, 'twill fray;
If to a plane-tree, 'twill be felled one day;
All girls are likened to gazelles thou'lt say—
How then shall I describe thee truly, love?

The violet is wild, and low of birth;
Rubies are stones, for all their priceless worth:
The moon itself is made of rocks and earth—
All flame, thou shinest like the sun, my love.

Thy door I seek as pilgrims seek a shrine:
Thine eyes are roses, new-blown eglantine;
Thy tongue a pen, thy hands like paper fine,
A flower fresh from the sea thou art, my love!

Within my soul thy hand has placed love's seed;
Thy wiles and coyness make my heart to bleed:
Thy Sayat Nova thou hast slain indeed,
Thine evil fate he bears for thee, my love.

CHRIST AND ABGARUS

From the History of Armenia,

by

MOSES OF KHORENE

ABGAR the son of Arsham began to reign in the twentieth year of the reign of Arshavr King of Persia. This Abgar was called the Great Man because of his exceeding meekness and wisdom. In the third year of his reign the whole of Armenia fell under the jurisdiction of Rome. . . . Therefore the Romans sent commissioners unto the land of Armenia who brought the image of Cesar and placed it in all the temples.

At this time was born our Savior Jesus Christ, the Son of God.

And there was a dispute between Abgar and Herod. For Herod commanded that his image also should be placed in the temples of Armenia, with that of Cesar; to which Abgar not acceding, the anger of Herod was kindled against him. And he sent his brother's son with a great army against him. And Abgar met and fought him; and he was slain in the battle and his army fled.

Soon after these things Augustus died, and Tiberius reigned over the Roman Empire; and Germanicus sent messengers from Rome unto Arshavr and Abgar concerning the battle in which Herod's brother's son was slain. Whereupon Abgar was displeased, and thought to prepare for revolt and war. Then did he build the city of Edessa wherein to keep the hosts of Armenia, and removed thither his court from Mdzpin, with all his idols: Nebog, Bel, Batnikol, and Tarata; also with the Royal Palace he removed the books of the schools belonging to the temples.

But strife had arisen between his kinsmen of the reigning house of Persia, and Abgar collected his armies and went to reconcile and pacify them. And having settled their disputes he returned home; not sound in his body, but tormented with a painful disease.

At that time Marinus was governor over Phoenicia, Palestine, Assyria, and Mesopotamia. And Abgarus sent two of his notables unto him to show him the treaty of peace between Arshavr and his brother (for the Romans suspected that he had been to Persia to collect armies against them). And Marinus received them with peace and great honor, sending word unto Abgarus, "Fear nothing, only hasten to raise all the taxes."

And on their return the messengers went up to Jerusalem to see our Savior Christ, having heard of His wonderful deeds.

And when they had seen Him with their own eyes they returned and told Abgar; at which the king marveled, and believed Him to be the very Son of God. And because His body was tormented with a painful disease contracted in the land of Persia seven years before, and he was not able to find any cure by men, he sent unto Him a letter asking Him to come and heal him of his disease.

The Letter of Abgarus to our Savior Jesus Christ.

"Abgarus, a prince of the world, unto Jesus, the Savior and Benefactor, Who hast appeared in the City of Jerusalem, greetings.

"I have heard of Thee and of the healings wrought by Thy hands, without drugs and without roots; for it is said that Thou givest sight to the blind, Thou makest the lame to walk, and Thou cleansest the lepers; Thou curest those who have been long tormented by diseases, and raisest even the dead. And when I heard all this concerning Thee I thought that either Thou art God come down from Heaven that workest these things, or the Son of God. I have written unto Thee that Thou shouldest trouble Thyself to come unto me, and heal me of my disease. I have heard also that the Jews murmur against Thee, and think to torture Thee. My city is a small one, but it is beautiful, and it is sufficient for us twain."

And taking the letter they found Him in Jerusalem. And unto this the gospel beareth witness, saying: "There were some amongst the heathen that came up to Him." But our Savior did not undertake to come at the time when they called Him, but made Abgarus worthy of a letter; thus:

The Answer to the Letter of Abgarus, written at the command of our Savior by the Apostle Thomas.

"Blessed is he who believeth on Me though he hath not seen Me. For it is written concerning Me thus: 'They that have seen Me believed not on Me, but they that have not seen Me shall believe and live.' And concerning that which thou hast written unto Me to come down unto thee, it is needful that I fulfill all that for which I was sent; and when I have fulfilled it I will ascend unto Him that sent Me. And after My ascension I will send one of My disciples, who shall heal thee of thy disease, and give Life unto thee and unto all them that are with thee."

This letter did Anan the messenger bring unto Abgarus, with the Image of the Savior, which remaineth in the city of Edessa until this day.

ARAXES CAME DEVOURINGLY

BY HOVHANNES HOVHANNESSIAN

ARAXES came devouringly,
Swept o'er her boulders scouringly—
Where shall I lay my aching head
Bowed down with grief o'erpoweringly?

Oh my Araxes, flow serene;—
Tell me, hast thou my sweet love seen?
My heart's desire is unfulfilled;—
Arax, hast thou more happy been?

Mount Ararat with clouds is veiled,
My love is lost, my hope has failed.
For pity's sake an answer give
To my sad heart with grief assailed.

I sob and weep the livelong night;
Till dawn I watch—I watch and write;
Arax, ere sunrise gild thy waves
To thee I bring my spirit's blight.

Upon the rocks the sunbeams dart,
Red flames devour my mourning heart;
Those eyes and brows have left with me
A sorrow which shall ne'er depart.

THE PARROT'S SONG

BY RAFFI

(1837-1888)

WITH nuts and sweets and dainty fare,
   My lady feeds me oft.
She decks my cage with tender care,
   And hands so white and soft.

But not a moment's joy can give
   This pampering care to me,
Since as a prisoner here I live,
   In gilded misery.

EARTH AND SKY

BY HOVHANNES TOUMANIAN

THE Sky bent down his piercing gaze one day
On Mother Earth, that far beneath him lay.
And as he looked on mountain, sea, and grove,
On hill and dale, he burnt with thoughts of love.

Earth lying numbed and frozen 'neath the snow,
Sudden awoke to springtime's ardent glow,
And flames of fire her beating heart consumed,
While myriad flowers the air around perfumed.

And thus they loved, though never side by side,
Though Nature willed they should be parted wide—
   The Earth and Sky.

But when has love accepted with content
An obstacle When o'er the earth steals night,
The starry Sky, his vision downward bent,
Opens his thousand eyes of shining light,
And gazes on his love in worship still,
Gazes till dawn, and cannot take his fill.

And as he gazes, all his starry eyes
Are strewn into Earth's breast of waters blue,
Which foam, and heave, and swell, and strive to rise,
Longing to reach and join her lover true.

He, more and more inflamed by passion's fire,
In all the splendors of the night arrayed,
Pours in her ear his longing and desire,
And shows her all his pomp and pride displayed;
   Towards her turning
   And ever yearning.

But when he finds his love is out of reach
He turns away, nor utters sound nor speech;

And in the dark the tears that dim his sight
Fall on earth's cheeks in showers of dewdrops bright,—
Dewdrops of pearl—the tears that heaven weeps,
And then Earth's bosom swells. Her thousand deeps,
Her boundless oceans, rise once more to meet
The far-off loved one; and her mountain peaks
Like myriad lips rise up the clouds to greet,—
To kiss their gloomy forms, and sullen cheeks.

And love torments her with its ceaseless fire.
Her waters foam, and writhe, and are convulsed,
Yet never may they reach their heart's desire,—
Restlessly sobbing, ever more repulsed.

   And from her gloomy throne,
   Behind the clouds, alone,
The moon beheld it with her sleepless eye.
And told the Poet how she did espy
That in the darkness of the silent night
Earth heaved her bosom up to Heaven above;
And that the sky smiled on her with delight,
As they exchanged the secret kiss of love;
And for each other sweetest songs they sing
And they embrace each other and caress,
Like living souls, each other gladdening.

Then on the Poet fell a deep distress,
A jealous sorrow—for he fain would, too,
Possess a love as noble and as true.

O'ER THE MOUNTAINS HIGH HE WENT

FOLK SONG

O'ER the mountains high he went,
    Love, love!
    In the meadows above
    I seek for my love.
With a weary sigh he went.
    Love, love!
    To fight thou art gone
    While I stay here alone.

Neither quail nor partridge stirred.
    Love, love!
    In the meadows above
    I look for my love
And he left without a word.
    Love, love!
    To fight thou art gone
    While I stay here alone.

Like a flower's fragrance sweet
He came past, and vanished fleet.
    I beheld him and I loved
    But we never more shall meet.

When my lover rode away
Not a farewell did I say;
    None there is to help him now —
    Sourb Carapet, [9] bless his way!

---

[9] The patron saint of lovers.

COMPLAINTS

BY BEDROS TOURIAN

FAREWELL, thou Sun, and Thou, O Power Divine,
That far above my spirit dimly shine.
I go to add another star to heaven:—
For what are stars, but anguished curses, riven
From innocent and hapless souls, that fly
To burn the brow of Heaven? and they supply
Fresh armaments, and jewels fiery red,
To God, the source of lightning flashes dread!

Alas, what do I say? Send forth thy fires,
O God! Consume this brain that thus aspires
To soar, and dares to pierce the depths of heaven;
And e'en to climb unto the stars has striven!

Creator of our trembling beings, hail!
Of light and youth, of age when forces fail;
Thou that the roses from my brow hast wrenched,
Hast stilled my trembling lips, my longings quenched;
Mist to mine eyes hast given, sobs to my breath:—
Yet thou hast sworn to smile on me in death!
Ah, surely thou hast kept for me a life
Of fragrance, light, and prayer beyond this strife!
But if my latest breath must perish here
All silently, in this dark atmosphere—
From now a flash of lightning I would be,
Coiled round thy name, and, murmuring ceaselessly,
A curse I would become to pierce Thy side—
God, the Arch Enemy, I would deride!

Ah me, I tremble, and am pale as death.
My brain seethes like a hell; a sobbing breath

I am amongst the mournful cypress trees,
An autumn leaf soon wafted by the breeze!

Oh, I would live!—give me of life one spark!
To dream—and then embrace the grave so dark?
My God, how black is this decree of doom
Writ in the lees of dread sepulchral gloom!
Oh, give my soul one drop of living fire—
To love—and live for ever I desire!
Ye stars of heaven, into my spirit fall
There live, and hear your hapless lover call!

To my pale brow the springtime brings no rose.
No smile for me in this world's sunbeams glows.
Night is my coffin, stars for lights flame round.
The moon all weeping seeks my funeral mound.
There are some men for whom no mourners sigh—
It was for them He placed that moon on high;
And he that to death's portals draweth near
First life would have—and then a mourner's tear.

In vain the stars of heaven spelt "Love" for me
And nightingales explained its mystery.
In vain of Love I learnt to know the truth,
And crystal waves reflected back my youth.
In vain the forest silent lay around—
The secret leaves gave forth no breath or sound;
They would not break upon my reverie—
They let me dream of Love eternally.
All, all in vain I saw the flowers of spring
Their incense to my dreams' fair altar bring;
With their delights they all have mocked at me—
And all the world is but God's mockery!

A DAY AFTER

BY BEDROS TOURIAN

SLUMBERING darkly yesterday[10]
As in deathly sweats I lay,
And two roses fiery red
On my faded cheeks were spread—
On my brow perchance a ray
Of Death's pallor trembling lay.
And I prayed and longed for death.
Then I heard a sobbing breath . . .
I unclosed my weary eyes
And beheld my mother's tears—
Saw those priceless pearls arise,
Tokens of her love, her fears.
In her heart what grief she bore!
And I was that anguish sore.
Ah, I raged tempestuously,
That black torrent outward leapt :—
God of mercy, pardon me,
For the tears my mother wept!

---

[10] The poem entitled "Complaints," written a few days before his death.

WITHOUT THEE WHAT ARE SONG AND DANCE TO ME?

BY SAYAT NOVA

WITHOUT thee what are song and dance to me?
The castagnettes I throw down wearily.
My heart and thoughts are ever filled with thee,
So rhymes and verses leave me, one by one.

How can one bandage serve for gashes twain?
How on two masters wait a single swain?
Would not one gardener tend two groves in vain?
For he must graft the saplings one by one.

Well said our fathers, speaking of such woes,
"I made a garden, others plucked the rose.
Theirs was the sweetness, mine the thorny close."
In sooth these things befell me one by one!

Without thee what are riches unto me?
What worth could I in silks or cashmeres see?
Arrayed in rags and sackcloth I would be,
Wandering around the convents, one by one,

To meet perchance with some one, who might tell,
My fair one, how to free me from thy spell;
For Sayat Nova's torments far excel
The Seven Wise Men's complaints told one by one!

THE LAKE OF VAN

BY RAFFI

UNUTTERABLE silence here is spread
On every hand, and Nature might be dead.
A lonely exile, here I sit and weep,
And far above, bright Moon, I see thee sweep.

From Earth's creation till the skies shall parch
And she dissolve, thou circlest Heaven's high arch:
Saw'st thou the laurels on Armenia's brow?
And dost behold her hopeless sorrows now?

Mournful as I! I wonder dost thou see
How she is ground by heels of tyranny!
And do thine eyes with bitter tear-drops smart
When barbèd arrows pierce her through the heart

Thy heart is stone, thy pity stark and cold,
For fields of innocent blood thou dost behold
Without a word, and o'er Armenia's land
Thy nightly compass of the dome hast spanned
With all the brightness that was thine of old.

.   .   .   .

O Lake, make answer! Why be silent more?
Wilt not lament with one whose heart is sore?
And you, ye Zephyrs, hurl the waters high
That I may feed them from a mourner's eye!

A garden once, luxuriantly fair,
Now is Armenia choked with thorn and tare:
Thou who hast seen her fortunes wax and wane,
Tell me, I pray thee! Must she thus remain?

Must this unhappy nation ever be
By foreign princes held in slavery?

Is the Armenian and his stricken race
Counted unworthy in God's judgment-place?

Comes there a day, comes there a season that
Shall hail a flag on topmost Ararat,
Calling Armenians, wheresoe'er they roam,
To seek once more their loved and beauteous home?

Hard tho' it be, O heavenly Ruler, raise
Armenia's spirit, and her heart's dark ways
Light with Thy knowledge: understanding so
The mystery of life, her works shall show
That all she does is ordered to Thy praise.

  . . . . . .

Then suddenly the surface of the lake
Grew luminous, and from its depths did break
A lovely maid that bore a lantern and
A lyre of shining ivory in her hand.
Was she an Angel in a strange disguise?
Was she a Houri fled from Paradise?
Nay, rather was she of the form and hue
Of the Armenian Muses!
    "Tell me true,
O Muse," I cried, "our people's destiny!
Speak of the Now and of the Yet-to-be!"

Then the sweet heavenly Spirit made reply,
"Wipe, O sad youth, the salt tears from thine eye!
I bring glad tidings: better days shall break,
New days of joy, that carry in their wake
The reign of God, Whose will is free and just:
A Golden Age again shall gild the dust!

"Armenia's Muses shall awake anew,
And her Parnassus bloom with vernal hue,
And the bright car Apollo whirls on high
Shall sweep the shadows from her clouded sky.

"For many a day, like thee, we mourned aloud
While the thick darkness wrapped her in its shroud:
Now, O beloved, may the weeping cease,—
To us has come the olive branch of peace!

"Cleanse from thy lute the rust that soils its string;
Hasten thee back, and, as thou goest, sing
Such joyful lays as yet may re-inspire
Hearts that are dead with new and tameless fire.
His Will is done; the Time is here; the Day
Dawns; and the Morning Star, so God doth say,
Shall be thy sign."
                    Then darkness fell again;
The vision fled; but long there did remain
An echo of the thrilling voice, that blended
With the wild waves whose depths she had descended;
And flowery perfumes filled the air like rain.

O message dear, and sweet prophetic strain!
What happiness is come to us, but Oh!
Beautiful Muse, yet one thing would we know—
Can a dead corpse rise up and live again?

                    Translated by G. M. Green.

SPRING

BY MUGGURDICH BESHIGTASHLIAN

(1829-1868)

O LITTLE breeze, how fresh and sweet
Thou blowest in the morning air!
Upon the flowers caressingly,
And on the gentle maiden's hair.
But not my country's breath thou art:
Blow elsewhere, come not near my heart!

O little bird among the trees,
The sweetness of thy joyful voice
Entrances all the Hours of Love,
And makes the listening woods rejoice.
But not my country's bird thou art:
Sing elsewhere, come not near my heart!

How peacefully thou murmurest,
O gentle, limpid little brook;
Within thy mirror crystal-bright
The rose and maiden bend to look.
But not my country's brook thou art:
Flow elsewhere—come not near my heart!

Although Armenia's breeze and bird
Above a land of ruins fly;
Although through mourning cypress groves
Armenia's turbid stream flows by,—
They are the sighing of her heart,
And never shall from mine depart!

THE FOX

FOLK SONG

THE fox ran up into the mill,
He raised his paws, and danced his fill.
    Brave Master Fox, 'tis but your due,
    In all the world there's none like you!

A peck of corn he ground that day,
Which on his back he bore away.

He ate the village chickens brown,
And trod the upland cornfields down.

The fox lies on his shaggy side,
His paws stretched out before him wide.

Sable and fox this fall we'll catch,
And for my son I'll make a match.

Alas, this year no price they made:—
My Hovhannes unmarried stayed!

THE SONG OF THE VULTURE

BY ELIA DEMIRJIBASHIAN

(1851-1908)

A GREAT black bird like to a great black cloud
Hovers forever o'er my spirit bowed.
He is my guardian angel, but alack!
Darker than night he is—than hell more black.

A fearful-looking bird, with wings wide spread,
Ill-omened as the Devil, and as dread;
He hovers round my wasted body, till
I wonder if I yet have life or will.

Upon his wings no spot of white appears,
His plumage black sheds horror down, and fears.
Black are his talons—sharp, like daggers fell;
And like a hound I hear him howl and yell.

His wide-spread pinions hide the light from me;
Heaven dark, and earth a dungeon black I see.
All is in shadow—air and earth and skies—
He even hides the lightning from my eyes.

I cannot see the paleness of my face,
I cannot see the maiden's smiling grace;
Black is the lake, the stars and lilies dark;
What was that cry? The bird's dread calling!—Hark!

I seem to totter on the brink of hell
And think the evil fowl my corpse can smell.
I seem to hear the goblins fight with him—
"Away with thee!—ours is this booty grim!"

But he is cruel, strong, and merciless—
This great black bird;—he heeds not my distress.
Ten years I've lived beneath his deadly wings—
Ten years unceasingly my death-bell rings.

Ten years ago one night it came to pass
On Moda's rock I sat and dreamed; alas,
My foe came to me—Carnal was his name:
He shouted, "Vain are Life and Love and Fame!"

Youthful I was, and armed with Love and Hope
I struggled. "Oh, my soul, arise and cope
With this thy foe, and vanquish him," I cried.
But 'twas in vain, as I full soon espied.

My sun and joy since then are on the wane.
My foe cries out, "I, only I, shall reign!
O'er all the universe none rules but me!"—
Then rose a Siren's voice alluringly. . . .

Nirvana and the flesh held me that hour:
God was asleep—my soul was in their power.
Then on the moon I saw a spot appear;—
It grew, and grew . . . my heart turned sick with fear.

I was as dead. The carrion-eating bird
Had left that heavenly corpse—the moon—allured
To earth by me. It sought my bosom where
The image of Christ crucified lay bare.

Beneath those evil wings I hopelessly
Roam over the earth;—my guardian angel he;
No more the cross I wear, nor in my breast
Dwells holy faith; 'tis death: death without rest.

Like to the moon, whether I wax or wane
Still am I lifeless, cursed with this bane.
I give the vulture of my flesh to tear,
And shiver when the name of "love" I hear.

While yet I live he is devouring me:
I cannot bear this pain—Oh, set me free!

I am not dead—Love still dwells with me here.
I am alive—and some call me the "Ner." [11]

Ah, gruesome bird, art thou not yet content
These ten long years my body to have rent?
Ah, vulture black—black earth and ebon sky,
'Tis time that I should lay me down and die.

---

[11] "Ner" — the Antichrist, concerning whom the Armenians have many traditions.

DANCE SONG

FOLK SONG

"I HAVE loved your winsome face,
And your never-fading grace.
If they give you not to me
May God send them black disgrace!"

"Mountain sorrel, fresh with dew,
Sweets I send and honey new;
Is a dainty maid like me
Fit to wed a youth like you?"

"You are arch, my little maid,
In four plaits your hair you braid,
Make no more pretence to me—
For you love me, I'm afraid!"

"Drive your plough ahead, and go;
Underneath it thistles grow.
You are reckless, young, and wild—
She is mad would wed you so!"

"Near your house a field I'll sow
And I'll stone the ill-starred crow.
When I have the girl I love
I'll let all my folly go."

"On its way the water flows,
Washing with its waves the rose.
My beloved amidst the youths,
Like a mighty fortress shows."

"In the vineyard you have grown,
Where the melon plants are sown,
Day and night upon my lute,
You I sing, and you alone."

"Sing a minstrel's song to me,
Or the blackbird's rhapsody;
All your praises I deserve,
And my bridegroom you shall be!"

BALLAD

BY RAFFI

DARK forests clothe the mountain-side,
    And o'er that mountain's lofty head
The heavens bend their arches wide,
    And, dome-like, round its summit spread.

A castle stood upon the steep,
    Enchanted by a witch's spell;
A maiden wept within the keep,
    Bound by the chains of slav'ry fell.

Alone and sad, the maiden fair
    Sat in her dark and narrow room.
No hope had she, but dire despair
    Had worn her heart with thoughts of gloom.

A minstrel passed—as it befell
    A singer, singing sweetest strains;
He broke the witch's evil spell,
    And loosed the gentle maiden's chains.

She ran to him and kissed his face,
    And said, "How I have longed for thee!
God, in His mercy and His grace,
    Hath sent thee here to set me free!"

And when, above the mountain steep,
    The moon shone out her silver light,
And when the stars began to peep,
    Twinkling and scatt'ring jewels bright,

The minstrel's love stole out unseen,
    With burning thoughts of her belov'd;
All through the woods so dark and green,
    Seeking, and seeking him, she roved.

A hut there was within that wood,
    Meet dwelling for some dervish old;
All lined with moss and leaves, it stood
    Protected from the rain and cold.

The minstrel lived within this nook,
    And sang alone beneath the trees.
His friend—Firdausi's wondrous book,
    His comrades—Sadi and Hafiz.

The Houri of the castle there
    Spent many happy days and nights—
Immortal souls in Jennet [12] fair
    Have never tasted such delights.

He wiped the tears by sorrow shed,
    And healed the wounds by sorrow wrought;
Like captive from a prison fled,
    Her cares and woes she soon forgot.

Broken and aged was her sire;
    A mighty Prince, the castle's lord,
To satisfy his heart's desire,
    Had reft her from him with his sword.

The Prince held office high at court,
And countless women, bright as day,
Lived in his harem's vile resort,
And slaves, more than my tongue can say.

His women, guarded day and night,
Caged in with iron bars he keeps;
But LOVE, more strong than despot's might,
Breaks through that cage, those bars o'erleaps.

---

[12] The Paradise of Mohammed, where the souls of the blest are waited upon by beautiful houris, and fed with delicious fruits.

NO BIRD CAN REACH THE MOUNTAIN'S CREST

BY HOVHANNES COSTANIANTZ

No bird can reach the mountain's crest.
There blow the winds that never rest;
And 'midst the stars that crown the height,
Saint Gregory's fair lamp shines bright.
    Ah, gentle brother, sweet and brave,
    That Light thy sword and spirit save!

How many rills the mountain yields!
Those rills are streams, that dew the fields.
My brother sweet, those rushing streams
Are like my longings and my dreams.
    Happy the maid that loveth thee!
    When shall thy heart's desire be?

See, in the South a tempest breaks—
A tempest howls, the leaflet quakes;
The bluebell hangs its petals bright,
The cock cries out with all his might.
    Like showers of gold comes down the rain
    Why comes my love not home again?

The Star of Light begins his course,
The brave one mounts upon his horse.
He drives his spurs into its flanks,
And rides away to join the ranks.
    Happy the maid that loveth thee,
    When shall thy heart's desire be?

There comes no news from far away,
Our brave ones rest not from the fray.
'Tis long that sleep my eyes doth flee—
Our foemen press unceasingly.
    'Tis long for sleep I vainly pray:
    There comes no news from far away.

THE NIGHTINGALE OF AVARAYR

BY LEO ALISHAN

WHENCE comest thou, my moon, gentle and still,
Spreading thy light o'er meadow, vale, and hill,
And o'er this patriarch, that lost in thought
The midnight plains of Avarayr has sought
Whereon our fathers, martyred for the right,
As giants fell, to rise as angels bright!
Com'st thou to spread upon their ashes cold
From yonder snowy cloud a pall of gold?
Or would'st thou bind around thy brow of light
A token of Armenia's life-blood bright?-
Or art thou still in awestruck wonder lost
To think how Vartan fell, with all his host;—
Leaving death's shadow in his foeman's breast,
Trusting his soul to God, he sank to rest!

And thou, Dughmood, that stained with blood I see
Winding amongst thy rushes sobbingly;
Thou breeze that from Magou's steep rock dost waft,
Or from great Ararat descendest soft;—
Thou too like me dost tremble, and thy wings
Listlessly bear thee on thy wanderings:
O'er hill and dale thou fliest, from wood to wood,
Till on this plain thou stay'st thy wings to brood;
Then bearest on this careworn heart's last sigh
To echo in Armenia ere it die!

O friend of aching hearts, soul of the rose,
That breakest with thy voice the night's repose;
Sing, little Nightingale, from yonder tree—
Armenia's deathless heroes sing with me!
From Thaddeus' convent as thy voice I heard,
Praying before the cross, my heart was stirred.
I hastened forth beneath thy magic spell
And found thee on the plain where Vartan fell.

Ah, Nightingale of Avarayr, they say
No bird art thou that nightly sing'st thy lay,
But Eghishe, the singer wondrous sweet,
That in the rose's heart Vartan dost greet.
The winter drives thee far away to mourn;
Spring's roses bid thee to Ardaz return,
In Eghishé's sad notes to sob and cry,
To call Vartan, and list for a reply.

If ever like the fainting Nightingale's
My voice with you, Togarmah's sons, prevails,—
Sons of those fathers virtuous and wise,
Who with their glories filled books, plains, and skies;—
If of Armenian blood one drop should flow
Within your veins, or make your hearts to glow;
Or if their glories past you too would share,
To Ardaz with the patriarch repair!

THOU ART SO SWEET

BY SAYAT NOVA

THOU art so sweet thou wilt not pain the minstrel singing
     songs to thee,
But when he loves thee thou dost frown—in vain he tells
     his wrongs to thee.

Love's fire is such, 'twill not consume—'twill burn, and
     burn, and ever burn:
If in that sea of flame I fall to cool me thou wilt never turn.

Alas, how shall the minstrel bear thy lightning gleams that
     pierce his heart?
No pact or treaty wilt thou make—a monarch absolute
     thou art.

If thou dost meet with mountains high like wax thou
     meltest them away;
If cities fair lie on thy path, their pride in ruins thou dost
     lay.

In sooth, no compact wilt thou make with him who sings
     these strains to thee:
Sayat Nova no credit hath when he would tell his pains to
     thee.

THE WANDERING ARMENIAN TO THE SWALLOW

BY C. A. DODOCHIAN

O SWALLOW, gentle swallow,
  Thou lovely bird of spring!
Say, whither art thou flying
  So swift on gleaming wing?

Fly to my birthplace, Ashdarag,
  The spot I love the best;
Beneath my father's roof-tree,
  O swallow, build thy nest.

There dwells afar my father,
  A mournful man and grey,
Who for his only son's return
  Waits vainly, day by day.

If thou shouldst chance to see him,
  Greet him with love from me;
Bid him sit down and mourn with tears
  His son's sad destiny.

In poverty and loneliness,
  Tell him, my days are passed:
My life is only half a life,
  My tears are falling fast.

To me, amid bright daylight,
  The sun is dark at noon;
To my wet eyes at midnight
  Sleep comes not, late or soon.

Tell him that, like a beauteous flower
  Smit by a cruel doom,
Uprooted from my native soil,
  I wither ere my bloom.

Fly on swift wing, dear swallow,
    Across the quickening earth,
And seek in fair Armenia
    The village of my birth!

Translated by Alice Stone Blackwell.

THE CHRIST-CHILD

BY SAINT GREGORY OF NAREK

(951-1009)

THE lips of the Christ-child are like to twin leaves;
They let roses fall when he smiles tenderly.
The tears of the Christ-child are pearls when he grieves;
The eyes of the Christ-child are deep as the sea.
Like pomegranate grains are the dimples he hath,
And clustering lilies spring up in his path.

Translated by Alice Stone Blackwell.

THE CASTLE OF ANOUSH [13]

BY RAFFI

"ANOUSH" in name, but full of bitterness in reality.

On one side of the road that leads from Tisbon to Ecbatana stands a steep, pointed crag. Its massive base rises from an extensive bed of rock, on which Nature has placed it as on a firm pedestal.

Not a handful of earth is to be found upon its denuded surface. Not a single plant grows on its hard, stony sides.

The burning rays of the southern sun have dried and baked it like an earthen vessel in the potter's ever-burning fire. From time immemorial that rock has ever been so. It happened one day that Farhat, the great Persian sculptor, passed at the foot of the rock with his pickaxe on his shoulder. He was aroused suddenly from the deep meditation in which he had been lost by the sound of horns and trumpets. He stopped. Grey-hounds and hawk-bearers appeared, gay and thoughtless riders burst into sight like a storm, then passed away from sight like a storm.

The dim, shadowy outline of a face remained in his heart; that vision stole away his peace of mind. Every day at the same hour he was to be seen on the road waiting,—waiting with the tenderest feelings of his heart aroused. The beloved vision would appear, and after throwing a careless glance at him would pass by like a flash of lightning.

He lost his peace of mind, abandoned his Art, and wandered like one beside himself in the solitudes of the mountains.

Days passed, weeks passed, and months passed. One day he was sitting there waiting. She appeared. But this time there were neither greyhounds nor hawk-bearers with her. She was alone,

---

[13] Anoush = Sweet.

with a number of her maidens. She urged her horse on and came up to Farhat.

"Hail, great Master," she said. " What has chained thee to these mountains—to the solitudes of these desert places I ever see thee here."

"The joy of sometimes seeing a transcendently beautiful vision light up the solitudes of these desert places," answered Farhat.

"Is thy love so great, then?" she asked, smiling.

"Who can help loving her that has not a peer amongst the immortals? Who can help loving her whose breath gives life, whose one glance confers eternal happiness? Do you think that the heart of him that is ever occupied with the stone and the chisel becomes so hardened that there is no room left in it for beauty?"

"I think not so. He that can give form and life to a shapeless stone, he that creates beautiful beings out of cold marble, cannot but love what is beautiful himself. But listen, Artist—to win the heart of the daughter of the Arian King requires great sacrifices." "I know that great goddesses require great sacrifices."

"I do not demand what is impossible—I only wish to try thy love. Look, Farhat, dost thou see yonder rock " and she pointed to the sharp crag. " Thou must create palaces for me out of that rock, so that I may look down from the summit with delight, and watch how the Tigris threads the beautiful plains of Assyria with its silvery curves, or how the tall palm-trees of Baghistan wave at the breathing of the gentle zephyrs. And in the heart of the rock thou must make storehouses for my treasures, and underneath there must be dwelling-places for my horses. When all this is ready I shall be thine."

She spoke, and rode away.

Years passed away. The pickaxe and hammer of the Master worked untiringly at the unyielding rock. The ceaseless sounds of

108

the heavy blows were to be heard day and night. The work was carried on successfully. Love strengthened the genius of the great Master, and the beauty of the Arian King's daughter fired him with enthusiasm. He made chambers, he made state-rooms, he made halls decorated with pictures, and out of the solid rock he created a palace of marvelous beauty. He made the walls of the apartments live with pictures carved in relief. In one place he sculptured the battles that the old heroes and giants of Iran had fought with devils and evil spirits; in another the glory and greatness of the ancient kings of Iran, and festivals celebrating their victories and deeds of prowess. He drew on the stone the valiant acts of ancestral kings, their virtues, and the benefits that they scattered over the land of the Arians. He worked all these wonders for the one being to whom he had devoted all the passion of his love. He worked them all so that she might be continually reminded of the glorious past of Iran, that her heart might continually be rejoiced with the noble pride that she was the descendant of a great dynasty born of the gods, which had always done god-like deeds.

She came and saw it all.

"It is very beautiful," she said, "but there is no water here—there are no trees. Make fountains for me that shall throw the water up higher than the clouds. Plant trees for me under whose shadow I may rest;—rest in thine arms!"

She spoke, and rode away.

He turned the courses of far distant streams and brought the water by underground channels to the very summit of the rock. He shaped the stone, dug out basins, and created silvery fountains. Day and night the never-ending supply of water rose out of the fountains, and dewed the surrounding plants with pearl-like drops. He leveled the surface of the rock, and covered it with earth brought from distant places. He planted trees and made lofty hanging gardens that looked as if they were growing in the air. Years passed. The trees grew and gave fruit, the flowers blossomed and filled the scented gardens with their gladdening perfumes. The birds came and filled the place with their happy songs. But she who was to have been the queen and pride of that beautiful paradise did not appear. One day the Master sat at the foot of the palace he had made, leaning his chin on his hand and looking sorrowfully down the road. A peasant came up singing, and sat down beside him to rest a little.

"Whence comest thou?" asked the Master. "Thou art fortunate in being so happy."

"From Tisbon," said the peasant. "And why should I not be happy when all the world is rejoicing?"

"What has happened?"

"Dost thou not know that in town the wedding has already been going on for seven days and seven nights? The wine is flowing in rivers, and there is no limit to the dainty fare. They are eating, drinking, and making merry. The whole town resounds with the strains of music, and the feet of the dancers are never weary. I also came in for my share of good things—I ate and drank as much as I could, and now I am taking home what will be enough for my wife and children for many weeks."

"Whose wedding is it?"

"The King's."

"To whom is he married?"

"To Anoush."

The Master spoke no more. He only started as one struck by lightning, then remained motionless. Then he rose and walked with weak, trembling steps towards the palace he had created. He looked around, and for the last time raised his sorrowful eyes to all the work that was the result of passionate love and beautiful Art. Then he entered into his work-room. His tools were lying about. He took up a heavy hammer and came out on to the narrow ledge. "She deceived me!" he said, and threw the hammer up into the air. It turned over and over, then fell on to his head. His warm blood sprinkled the wonders that were the work of his hands.

Farhat did not obtain the desire of his heart, but the name of his beloved Anoush remained with that stone fortress, and it was called the Castle of Anoush.

That rock-hewn palace which was prepared to be the temple of love and everlasting happiness became a hell full of tears and unending suffering. It was there that the Kings of Persia imprisoned the Armenian Kings who fell captive into their hands.

HAPPINESS

BY ARSCHAG TCHOBANIAN

(Born 1872)

WEARY of vainly seeking Happiness
In city alleys full of sound and strife,
I hastened from the noisy human press,—
The labyrinth of this dark, groveling life.

I said, "The mountain knows its place of rest,"
And clambered up above the level plain;
But the bald Titan answered me distressed:—
"Dullness alone doth Time for me ordain."

I left the mountain and approached the winds—
Those infinite, proud spirits, ever free;
"We are the sighs of griefs that to your minds
Must still remain unknown," they answered me.

And then above the winds and clouds I rose,
Soared to the skies, and asked the stars of Heaven.
"We are the tears that flow from countless woes,"
The answer by those eyes of darkness given.

Above the stars, in the lone fields of space,
I saw God musing, sorrowful and mild.
"Father," I cried, "where is Joy's dwelling-place?"
He said, "I also do not know, my child."

CONCERNING DEATH

BY HOVHANNES TULKOURANTZI

(1450-1525)

O EVIL man, with passions fraught,
How long wilt thou strive after sin
Enough the ill that thou hast wrought:
Repent,—a holier life begin.

From Adam's time until this day,
No soul hath had immortal breath;
Thou heed'st not what the Scriptures say—
The sinner's punishment is death.

He that had palaces of gold,
And brilliant cities, fortress-bound,
Hath left behind his wealth untold,
And lies beneath the sodden ground.

Who loved to quaff the spicy wine,
And spent his life in ribaldry,
I saw him like a swollen swine,—
A loathsome corpse, unsavory.

The man that rode an arch-necked steed
And flashed his sword around to slay,
I saw him penitent indeed:—
Between two wooden planks he lay.

And evil wenches, women fair,
Who dress in robes of gaudy dye,
Who love to curl and braid their hair—
Their brightness with the sun might vie:

They swing about, and turn, and sway,
And are beloved of every man;
But hateful when Death comes are they,
To all who would their features scan.

113

Christ sits upon the throne of Light,
Rewarding those who loved His Word,
Crowning the just with glory bright
And penitents His voice that heard.

Ah, Hovhannes Tulkourantzi,
Listen with open heart and ear;
Seek out some way diligently
To win the crown of glory there.

LOVE ONE ANOTHER

BY BEDROS TOURIAN

UNDYING Love, Whose beams forever glow
On rose-red Golgotha's stupendous brow;
Wilt Thou those shafts still in Thy bosom keep?
What guardest Thou?—bones, spectres, chasms deep,—
That in the echoes of the mountain-side
Thy noble words, "Love one another," died?

Effaced and trampled is the poor man's tomb;
The poor man's candle flickers out in gloom;
And in that darkness starving children weep,
While in the palace revels high they keep.
The rich man's carriage dashes gaily past,
The beggar's lonely corpse to earth is cast.

The pallid angel of Gethsemane
Tears doth not heed nor flowers, nor glory's plea.
The poor find rest in his cold arms alone,
For in Death's shroud the high and low are one.
Though lightning-winged the winds cry o'er the moor,
"Love one another," here none love the poor.

ARMENIA:

ITS EPICS, FOLK-SONGS, AND MEDIAEVAL POETRY

BY ARAM RAFFI

Introduction

THE country that is called Armenia consists of a large plateau, covered with numerous mountain ranges, which are intersected by many valleys and passes, as well as by rivers and lesser streams of considerable depth. The climate differs in various parts of the country, the meteorological conditions ranging from frost and snow to extreme heat. Over the plains towers Mount Ararat, on which, as we read in the Bible, the Ark rested after the Flood. Here also is the traditional site of the Garden of Eden, and the four rivers mentioned in Genesis as rising in the Garden still flow through the Armenian land.

The origin of the Armenian people is enveloped in mystery, but it is an established fact that Armenia has had a civilization of its own from a very early date, and that the Armenians are one of the most ancient races in the world. They have had their periods of independence, but, on account of its geographical position, Armenia has seldom figured as one of the great ruling states of the world, although it has repelled by arms invasions of such nations as Assyria. Assyrian records are filled with descriptions of conflicts with Armenian kings; King Assur Nazir Haban (1882-1857 B.C.) gives this account of one of his "victories":—"They (the people of Ararat, or Urardu) fled to the impregnable mountains so that I might not be able to get at them, for the mighty summits were like drawn swords pointing to the skies. Only the birds of heaven soaring on their wings could reach them. In three days I was there, spreading terror in places where they had taken refuge. Their corpses, like autumn leaves, filled the clefts. The rest escaped to distant inaccessible heights."

Notwithstanding the boasts of the Assyrian kings, they did not succeed in permanently crushing the independence of Armenia.

Tigranes the Great brought Armenia more in contact with distant foreign lands. In his time his country began to be considered of importance by Greek and Roman historians. The Romans sent Lucullus to engage in war with Tigranes in order to crush his growing power. This is what—according to Plutarch—Lucullus said of Tigranes:—

"In Armenia Tigranes, King of Kings, is seated, surrounded with that power which has wrested Asia from the Parthians, which carries Grecian colonies into Media, subdues Syria and Palestine, cuts off the Seleucid and carries their wives and daughters into captivity." Cicero says of Tigranes the Great:—"He made the Republic of Rome tremble before the prowess of his arms."

To give even a short outline of Armenian folklore and poetry it is essential to point out those agencies and influences which have served to originate that literature. Hence its literature and history, like those of all countries, are interwoven. Notwithstanding its periods of greatness, Armenia was unable, as we said above, to continue to be a powerful and independent state. Thus we see Armenia serving as a bridge between armies engaged in war, and such has been its fate in all periods, even up to the present time.

It fell successively under the dominion of Assyria, Babylonia, and, finally, of Persia when, after the time of Cyrus, the kingdom of Persia was extended by Darius over nearly the whole of Asia. Although Armenia became a tributary of Persia, it still had its own independent king.

The Median Empire had been founded probably in 677-672 B.C. From that time Iranian influence was strongly felt in the politics, language, and social organization of Armenia, and the Iranian religion, with its terminology, names of divinities, and many folk-beliefs, permeated Armenian paganism.

Moreover, the Armenians, being the near neighbors of the Persians, closely resembled them in their manner of life and their religion. After the conquest of Alexander the Great, Armenia, like all other Asiatic nations, fell under Greek dominion. Then the Macedonian rule gave way to the Parthian, and the dynasty of the Arsacidae held sway, a king of that race being set over Armenia and founding an independent Armenian dynasty. The Arsacidae introduced Greek civilization and culture into Armenia. During this period the character of the Armenians changed. Not only their religion but their manners and customs became different from those of the Persians. The rule of Macedonia over Armenia lasted 180 years (330-150 B.C.). The Graecophile Arsacid dynasty lasted 376 years (150 B.C.-226 A.D.). These long periods brought the Armenians into close contact with the Greeks and separated them from the Persians.

Armenian Paganism

To the periods which we have outlined belongs the literature of Armenia preceding the introduction of Christianity. Of this literature the remains that have come down to us consist of legends, songs, and fragments of epics. Of the epics we have some records and summaries, chiefly found in the History of Moses of Khorene (5th century A.D.), who has also preserved some of the heroic songs in their original form. These epics relate the history of Armenian ancestral and mythical heroes, to whom are ascribed the foundation and development of the Armenian nation. In them we see Armenian ideals of the earliest times. As these ideals are closely interwoven with the religious beliefs of the pre-Christian period, let us now cast a glance at Armenian Paganism.

It is said by ancient Armenian historians that the Armenians were originally worshippers of the One True God, but they, like all other nations, deserted Him and took up with various religions. Sun-worship was one of these; Zoroastrianism also had its turn; in due course, the Greeks introduced their own deities; even India succeeded in making its influence felt. Strabo has it that the Armenians, during the period of the Arsacid dynasty, were of the same religion as the Parthians. It appears that the

118

Armenians fused together Zoroastrianism and the polytheism of Greece and other nations, thus combining eastern and western religion. One result of this fusion was that though the Zoroastrians made no visible representation of their God, the temples of Armenia were full of images, brought from Mesopotamia, Asia Minor, and Greece.

The principal god of Armenia was Aramazd, whom the Armenians called "the Architect of the Universe, Creator of Heaven and Earth." He was also the father of the other gods. The Armenians annually celebrated the festival of this god on the 1st day of Navasard,[14] when they sacrificed white animals of various kinds—goats, horses, mules, with whose blood they filled goblets of gold and silver. The most prominent sanctuaries of Aramazd were in the ancient city of Ani in Daranali, the burial-place of the Armenian kings, as well as in the village of Bagavan in Bagravand.

Aramazd had an attendant incorporeal spirit, named Tir or Grogh ("writer"), whom he sent to earth to watch men and record in a book their good and evil deeds. After death, human souls were conducted by Tir to Aramazd, who opened the book at each soul's record, in accordance with which he assigned a reward or punishment. In a village near Vargharshapat there was a temple of this god, where the priests interpreted dreams after consulting his oracle. The influence of Tir was great in Armenia, for he was a personification of hope and fear. There are traces of the cult of this god in the Armenian language. It is still usual to hear, used as a curse, the expression, "May Grogh take you!" The son of Aramazd was Mihr, Fire. He guided the heroes in battle and conferred wreaths on the victors. The word mehian ("temple") is derived from Mihr; also some Christian names. One of the months in the ancient Armenian calendar (Mehekan) was named after him. His commemoration-day was celebrated with great splendour at the beginning of spring. Fires were kindled in the open market-place in his honor, and a lantern lighted from one of these fires was kept burning in his temple throughout the year. This custom of kindling fires in the spring is still observed

---

[14] Navasard fell, according to the later calendar of pagan Armenia, in August

in some parts of Armenia.

Although the Persians and the Armenians were both worshippers of Mihr, the conceptions and observances of the two nations differed. The Armenian sacred fire was invisible, but the Persian was material and was kept up in all the temples. For this reason the Armenians called the Persians fire-worshippers. But the Armenians had also a visible fire-god, who, although material, was intangible—the sun—to which many temples were dedicated and after which one of the months (Areg) was named. [15]

Long after the introduction of Christianity, there was a sect of sun-worshippers existent in Armenia, who were called "Children of the Sun." A small remnant of them is still supposed to be found, dwelling between the Tigris and the Euphrates. Traces of sun-worship are also evident in the Armenian language and in the Armenian literature of Christian times. Some sayings and phrases are still in use which contain references to sun-worship, such as the expression of endearment, "Let me die for your sun!" and the oath, "Let the sun of my son be witness."

One of the most famous Armenian goddesses was Anahit, who answered to the Greek Artemis and the Roman Diana. She was a " pure and spotless goddess," and, as a daughter of Aramazd, was "mother of chastity," as well as the benefactress of the whole human race; "through her the Armenian land exists, from her it draws its life; she is the glory of our nation and its protectress"[16]; and for her the ancient Armenians felt intense love and adoration.

Many images and shrines were dedicated to her under the names of "the Golden Mother," [17] "the Being of Golden Birth," etc. Every summer there was a festival in her honor. On that day, a dove and a rose were offered to her golden image, whence the day was called Vardavar, which means "the flaming of the Rose." On the

---

[15] Annual bonfires are kindled by Armenians on the festival of Candlemas, or the Purification of the Blessed Virgin Mary (February 13/2).

[16] *Agathangelos.*

[17] Statues of massive gold were consecrated to her, one of which was captured by the soldiers of Antony (Pliny, *H. N.*, XXX. 24).

introduction of Christianity, the temple of Anahit was destroyed and her festival became the Feast of the Transfiguration of Christ; it falls in the last days of the year according to the ancient Armenian calendar; but the name "Vardavar" still remains and doves are still set flying on that day. This is also the Armenian "water-day," during which the people amuse themselves throwing water at each other.[18]

Anahit was sought also in cases of great sickness.

The sister of Anahit was Astghik, [19] the goddess of beauty, a personification of the moon, corresponding to the Phoenician and Sidonian Astarte. Strange to say, the Persians had no goddess of beauty, but the bright sky of Armenia, its numerous valleys, the torrents running down from snow-capped mountains, the lakes, the cultivated fields and meadows tended to strengthen the sense of beauty, and, therefore, Armenia had a goddess of beauty, who was not to be found in the pantheon of the neighboring country.

The Armenians assigned Astghik a husband worthy of her. He was Vahagn, deified on account of his valour. In ancient songs, he is credited with a miraculous birth. The fires of heaven and earth, and the sea crimson in the light of dawn, travailed to bring him into being. [20] As we shall see later, Moses of Khorene has preserved portions of these songs. Vahagn was called Vishapakagh (Uprooter of dragons), as he cleared the Armenian land of monsters and saved it from evil influences. His exploits were known not only in Armenia, but in the abode of the gods.

---

[18] At each festival, the Armenians had to show what progress they had made during the past year, in art and in other occupations, and races and other competitions took place, the victors being crowned with wreaths of roses. When the doves were set flying the High Priest sprinkled the people with the waters of the Aradzani--a tributary of the Euphrates--and the people in their turn sprinkled each other. The customs dated back to traditions of the deluge--that universal baptism with which God cleansed all the sinful earth, and the same expression of love and forgiveness is manifested in the presence of the dove at the baptism of Jordan. See Raffi's *Samuel*, chap. ix.

[19]*Astghik* means in Armenian "little star."

[20] It is a curious coincidence that Venus, the Greek goddess of beauty, was also the wife of a fire-god, Vulcan.

Having stolen corn from the barns of King Barsham of Assyria, he ran away and tried to hide himself in heaven. From the ears he dropped arose the Milky Way, which is called in Armenia the Track of the Corn-stealer.

The third daughter of Aramazd was Nané or Nooné. She was the goddess of contrivance. It was believed by the Armenians that contrivance was a necessary power for a woman, because, in the management of the household, she had to make big things out of small ones, and circumstances were already against her on account of the vicissitudes which Armenia was constantly undergoing.

Sandaramet, the wife of Aramazd, was an invisible goddess and a personification of the earth. Aramazd sent rain upon her, which brought forth the vegetation on the earth. She came to be a synonym of Hades and was very frequently referred to as such in theological books and in the hymnary of the Christian Church.

Besides these gods of their own, the Armenians also adopted alien divinities. When Tigranes brought a number of Phoenicians to Armenia as prisoners, they brought with them their god Ammon, from whose name comes the word Ammonor, [21] "the day of Ammon"—the New Year. Assyrian, Arab, and other emigrations also led to the introduction of foreign deities. An Armenian king, when he brought home captives, also introduced the gods of those captives, whose images were placed in the temples beside those of the native gods that they most closely resembled. Even Indian fugitives brought the brother-gods, Demetr and Gisanes, whose images were not like those of the other gods of Armenia, for the images of the gods of Armenia are, as a rule, small, whereas these were very tall, with long black hair and black faces. There was also a great immigration of Jews into Armenia, and this influenced the Armenians in the direction of monotheism. Besides the principal gods, there were also secondary ones. These were spirits, corresponding to angels, who acted as guardians to different classes of natural objects:—

---

[21] Some say that *Ammanor* was an ancient Armenian god and not foreign.

Kadjk, [22] who occupied the mountains; Parik, who presided over flocks; and many others.

Water was honored in Armenia as a masculine principle. According to Tacitus (Annals, vi. 37) the Armenians offered horses as sacrifices to the Euphrates, and divined by its waves and foam. Sacred cities were built around the river Araxes and its tributaries. Even now there are many sacred springs with healing powers, and the people always feel a certain veneration towards waters in motion.

There were gods who lived in the waters and destroyed harmful monsters of the deep. There was also a god who breathed out a mysterious atmosphere which destroyed malignant creatures. One wonders whether this is a foreshadowing of the fear of microbes. All the gods of this class were friendly to agriculturists.

There were also "Haurot-Maurot," the name of a flower (hyacinthus racemosus Dodonei) first mentioned by Agathangelos. The Arabs incorporated them in the Quran (ii. 96) as two angels sent down to live in Babel in human circumstances.

Alk, who dwelt in the waters, was a very harmful devil. He used to live in the corners of houses and stables, and in damp places. He had eyes of fire, nails of copper, teeth of iron, and the jaws of a wild boar. He carried a sword of iron in his hand and was a bitter enemy to pregnant women, near whom he sat at the time their child was born.

There were nymphs, who were guardians of women. They wandered through gardens and amid streams, but were invisible. They attended weddings and frequented bathrooms and the women's quarters in general. These nymphs and spirits were innumerable. Every woman was supposed to have a guardian nymph. The nymphs were supposed by some to be immortal and endowed with perpetual youth; others described them as mortal though they never grew old. There was also a group of male spirits who were regarded by some as mortal, by others as

---

[22] *Kadjk* means in Armenian "brave ones."

immortal. They wandered with the nymphs through forests, gardens, and other open places. They were imagined as very tall, with features like those of men; some were half-man and half-animal. Some were called Parik, "dancers"; others Hushka parik, "dancers to a melody in a minor key."

In some places, even now, a belief in these nymphs (or fairies) survives. Many stories are told of their beauty, their marvellous dancing, and their wondrous music. They are never called by the name of "nymphs," but are spoken of by the people of the country as "our betters." Still in some parts of Armenia, in May and October, a festival is held annually in honor of them, generally by the women in the Public Baths. They assemble early in the morning and remain till late at night, dancing, eating, and bathing.

Before the people thought of building temples, they worshipped their gods in forests and on mountains. One of these forests was the Forest of Sos. According to tradition the son of Ara the Beautiful, Anushavan, who devoted himself to the worship of this sacred place, was called, after the forest, Sos. The priests derived oracles from the rustling of the leaves in this holy wood.

Besides temples, which were numerous in Armenia, there were, all over the country, altars and shrines, as well as images and pictures.

To sum up, the pre-Christian religion of Armenia was at first a kind of nature-worship, which developed into polytheism. There were two elements in Armenian religion, the native and the foreign.

Besides nature-worship, there was a recognition, among the Armenians, of the Good and Evil Spirit, but predominance was given to the former. It is curious that, in the Armenian pantheon, there is no god of evil, and Armenian epic heroes are always described as fighting against evil spirits.

Armenian Epics

In Armenian epics, the immortals stand in the background, the most prominent place being assigned to legendary heroes, to whom poets attribute divine descent, thus tracing the origin of the Armenian race to the gods. Unfortunately, the greater part of these epics is lost, though a few fragments are preserved, in their original shape, by Moses of Khorene.

The following is one of these fragments, which gives the general conception of the gods and the heroes descended from them:—

"Glorious and awful were the former gods. They were the cause of the greatest blessings of the earth; also of the beginning of the world and the generations of men. From them arose a race of giants, with great limbs, fantastical, of stupendous stature, who, in their arrogance, conceived the impious idea of tower-building. But by the wrath of the gods, a mighty wind arose, overthrowing and shattering the structure. The speech of men was confused; there was general bewilderment."

Among the giants mentioned in this passage was Haik, the brave and illustrious chief—a famous archer, who is the patronymic hero of Armenia, and is described by Moses of Khorene as having curly hair and being beautiful to look upon, with brawny arms, well-set shoulders, and fiery eyes. Recoiling from submission to Belus, he, with his followers, went northwards to the foot of a mountain, where they took up their abode. Belus sent emissaries to him, bearing the following message:—

"Thou hast departed and hast settled in a chill and frosty region. Soften thy hard pride, change thy coldness to geniality; be my subject, and come and live a life of ease in my domain. Thus shalt thou find pleasure."

Haik's answer was to prepare for combat. The fights between Haik and Belus are minutely recounted. The dress of the two champions, their looks, their weapons, are all described in detail. At last Belus was vanquished and slain by his adversary.

Before the time of Moses of Khorene, Haik was known as a great hunter like the Greek Orion. In the passages in Job and Isaiah where "Orion" appears in the English Bible as the name of a constellation, "Haik" appears in the Armenian version.

The country that Haik conquered was named Hayastan, after him.

He was succeeded by Armenak, who extended the boundaries of his kingdom. This expansion is thus described by Moses of Khorene:—

"Armenak, taking with him all his host, goes to the north-east. He descends on a plain surrounded by high mountains, through which, from the west, murmuring streams flow. The plain extends towards the east. From the foot of the mountains gush springs no less limpid, mingling together to form little rivers, which, with gentle flow, run round the edge of the plain, parallel to the base of the mountains.

"But the southern mountain, with its white peak, at first rises straight up; afterwards it curves, looking beside the other heights like a hoary stooping elder amid youths."

Armenak was succeeded by Aramais. This king took up his abode on a hill beside a river, where he built a town which he named Aramavir. The river he called by the name of his grandson, Araxes. He had a son, named Shara, who was a glutton and had an immense number of children. He sent him to a very fertile place which was called, after him, Shirak.

Moses of Khorene quotes a proverb relating to Shara:—"If thou hast the gullet of a Shara, our stores are not the stores of a Shirak."

Shara had a son, Amasa. After him Mount Ararat was named "Masis."

Moses of Khorene mentions another descendant of Haik, whose name was Tork. He was ugly and of tremendous strength. He was

126

able to break great stones with his hands. Once, when he was on the shore of the Sea of Pontus, he hurled huge rocks at the ships of his enemies and sank them. This incident reminds us of the Cyclops Polyphemus, in the Odyssey. Tork had also artistic proclivities. After dividing large stones with his hands, he smoothed them with his nails, and with his nails covered them with drawings of eagles and other pictures.

Then the historian gives a table of royal names down to Aram, whom he describes as industrious and patriotic, and who said that he would rather die for his fatherland than endure the sight of strangers devastating it. He collected an army of 50,000 and drove the foreign invaders out of Armenia. Epic poems, according to Moses of Khorene, praise Aram's valour in his conflicts with Barsham, King of Assyria, whom he eventually subdued. He was succeeded by Ara the Beautiful.[23]

The romantic love of Semiramis for this king, which was a favourite theme of ancient Armenian song and epic, is elaborately recounted by Moses of Khorene. A translation of his narrative is given on page 27 of this volume. There are several variants of this story, which is still related in Armenia, and the names of many places as well as many superstitions can be traced to it.

Semiramis invited Ara to Nineveh to be her husband, promising him the half of the kingdom, but Ara refused her offer, having a wife already. Semiramis thereupon sent an army against Ara, with orders to capture the king alive and bring him to her; but, instead of the living king, they brought his corpse. Semiramis, who, as is well known, was accustomed to practice magic, laid the body on a certain high place, in order that the gods might descend and restore it to life by licking the wounds. This height is still called Lezk, and in former times others used it for the same purpose as Semiramis: The idea of this mode of cure probably originated from the fact that wounded men, lying unconscious on the battlefield, have often been revived by the licking of dogs and

---

[23] Zarmayr, another king of this dynasty, took part in the defense of Troy. The historian emphasizes the fact that he was killed by Achilles himself.

other animals.

In Moses of Khorene we find this story about the childhood of Sanatruk. One day, he, under the care of his mother and his nurse, was walking among the mountains of Kordua, when suddenly a high wind arose, accompanied by a snowstorm, and separated the mother from her son. For three days and nights the nurse and the child were buried in the snow, but the gods sent a miraculous white animal which rescued them and brought them home alive. [24]

But, though such legends as these may have some foundation in fact, there are others that are entirely fabulous, like the following, which is related by Moses of Khorene:—

The heir to the principality of Ardzruni, when a boy, fell asleep in the open air. A storm of rain came on and drenched him; and then the hot sun shone down and scorched him with its rays; whereupon an eagle flew up and hovered over his head with outspread wings, sheltering him from the assaults of nature.

In the fourth century A.D., we find a similar story told of Prince Mushegh Mamikonian. After his death his relatives put his body on a high tower, believing that the spirits would descend and restore him to life. This story is found in Faustus Byzand (A.D. 337-384).

The animals figuring in such stories as these are not represented as merely adjuncts to man, but as independent individuals who act in accordance with their own characters and inclinations. Plato, in his Republic, gives a slightly different version of the legend of Ara. Er was an Armenian (or, as some commentators say, "The son of Armenios"), a native of Pamphylia. He was slain

---

[24] It is interesting to recall, in this connection, some passages of Strabo. Speaking of Armenia he says:--"It is said that people passing by the foot of the mountains are often buried in the snow which falls from the summits. In order to be prepared for such a mishap, travelers carry with them two long sticks for the purpose of making breathing places for themselves, should they be covered by the snow. The sticks, at the same time, serve as signals to any other travelers who may happen to be passing."

in battle, and ten days afterwards, when the bodies of the dead were taken up, already in a state of corruption, his body was found unaffected by decay and carried away home to be buried. And on the twelfth day, as he was lying on the funeral pile, he returned to life and told them what he had seen in the other world.

The name "Er" is evidently a variant of Ara. The story, as told by Plato, has all the features of a transplanted legend.

Moses of Khorene says that, after the death of Ara the Beautiful, Semiramis passed the rest of her days in Armenia, which place she greatly loved. Here she established the city of Van. The following account is given of the end of Semiramis:—

Being pursued by her enemies, she ran away on foot, and, becoming thirsty, she stopped to drink water from the Lake of Van. Here she was overtaken by the "swordsmen," whereupon, after taking off her magic bracelet and throwing it into the lake, she herself was turned into stone.

With regard to the bracelet of Semiramis, the following story is even now commonly told in the neighborhood of Van:—

Once Semiramis saw a bracelet in the hands of some little boys, who had found it in the river, and were examining it with curiosity. Semiramis, knowing that the bracelet had magic powers, took it away from the children. By means of this jewel, she allured youths to their destruction. This licentiousness brought her into general disfavor. An old man, at last, snatched the bracelet from her and ran with it towards the sea. Semiramis rushed after him in a fury, but, not being able to come up with him, she let down her long hair and used it as a sling to hurl a great rock at him. The weight of the rock pulled out her hair. The rock itself fell into a ditch near Artamet. Semiramis, through fear and amazement, was turned into stone. The old man threw the bracelet into the Lake of Van. Even now a rock is shown at Artamet which bears the name of "the Rock of Semiramis."

Then Moses of Khorene speaks of Tigranes I., who, in

129

conjunction with Cyrus, put an end to the kingdom of Media. The epics say of Tigranes that "his face was of lovely hue, his eyes were soft and lustrous, his shoulders stalwart, the calves of his legs were well-shaped, he was altogether fair to look upon; in food and drink he was moderate; he was of lofty mind, eloquent in speech, and masterly in the conduct of affairs. Just and equitable, he weighed each man's acts in the scale of his mind. He was not jealous of the great nor did he despise men of low estate, but spread the mantle of his care over all men alike. He increased our treasures of gold, silver, and precious stones. Under him, men and women wore fine garments, of divers colors, richly embroidered, which made the ill-favored to look fair and the beautiful to look like demigods.

"Tigranes, the bringer of peace and prosperity, caused all men to grow fat with butter and honey. In his day, the infantry became cavalry, slingers became skilful archers, dagger-bearers were equipped with swords, and naked soldiers were provided with shields and armor."

The historian adds that the splendor of the arms and equipments was enough of itself to drive back the enemy.

As the head of a band of warriors, he performed many valorous deeds:—"We were under the yoke of others, but he put other nations under our yoke and made them our tributaries."

His rival, Astyages, King of Media, was always suspicious and distrustful of him.

One night Astyages had a terrible dream. The next morning he summoned his courtiers. They found him sighing, looking on the ground with gloomy mien, and heaving groans from the depths of his heart. " When the courtiers inquired the reason of his behavior" (continues the historian) " the king remained silent for hours, then in a sad voice he related his dream, which was as follows:—

"'To-day I was in an unknown country, close to a mountain, which rose very high above the ground; its summit was covered with ice. It seemed to me to be in Armenia. After I had gazed for a long time, it appeared to me that there was a woman sitting on the summit. Her garments were purple. Her face was covered by a blue veil. Her eyes were beautiful. She was tall, with rosy cheeks. She was in travail, and for a long time I looked on her with admiration, then I beheld her give birth to three heroes, all of equal stature: the first, sitting on a lion, soared towards the west; the second, seated on a leopard, went towards the north; the third, bridling a huge dragon, defiantly attacked our kingdom. In these confused dreams, I seemed to be standing on the roof of my palace, and the covering of my chambers was adorned with beautiful fountains of variegated colors. The gods that had crowned me were standing there, with wondrous faces, and I, with you, was honoring them with incense and sacrifice. Suddenly looking up, I saw the man who was seated on the dragon wing his course in our direction, desiring to overthrow our gods. I advanced to the attack and engaged in fight with that youthful hero. First of all, with lances we pierced each other's bodies, calling forth rivers of blood, and past our sunlit palace flowed a crimson sea. For hours we fought also with other arms. But, to be brief, the fight ended in my defeat. I was bathed in sweat, sleep forsook me, and ever since I have felt as if I had no life in me. For all these visions signify that the Armenian king, Tigranes, is about to attack us. And whosoever amongst you, by counsel or deeds, wishes to aid me, and aspires to the honor of being a king, equal to myself, let him speak.'"

Then the story goes on to tell how Astyages, in order to prevent Tigranes from making war on him, proposed that his rival's sister, Tigranuhi, should be his wife; therefore Astyages sent to Tigranes one of his councilors with a letter accompanied by many precious gifts. Moses of Khorene gives the letter, which runs as follows:—

"Thou knowest, beloved brother, that of all the gifts of the gods to us none is more precious than the multitude of our dear ones, especially when they are wise and valiant. The reason of this is that, in such case, quarrels will not arise from outside, and if they arise, they will be unable to make their way within and will disperse themselves. Having seen the great advantage of such

131

relationships, it has entered my mind to confirm and strengthen the love that is between us, so that, both of us being secured on all sides, we may be able to carry on the affairs of our kingdom in greater safety. All this will be ensured, if thou wilt give me to wife thy sister Tigranuhi, the Great Lady of Armenia. I hope that thou wilt look favorably on this proposal, that she may be the Queen of Queens. Mayest thou have a long life, fellow sovereign and dear brother."

We have presented this letter as a matter of curiosity, because in none of the early European epics are there texts of letters. This usage is characteristically oriental. In Isaiah we read of the letter of Sennacherib to Hezekiah; there is also a letter in the Persian Firdusi's Shah-nameh.

After his marriage with Tigranuhi, Astyages tried to set her at enmity with her brother, and once he contrived cunningly to entice Tigranes to become his guest in order that he might slay him. But his wife perceived his treachery and secretly sent a message to her brother. Tigranes accepted the invitation of Astyages, but came accompanied by a great army. He postponed his attack till his sister had made her escape. In the battle which ensued, Astyages was killed.

Of this Tigranes, Xenophon says a great deal in his Cyropaedia, from which we cite the following incident:—

The Armenian king having revolted against Cyrus, the latter invaded Armenia and conquered him. Cyrus intended to deal very severely with the rebel monarch, but Tigranes, the son of the Armenian king, persuaded him to be more lenient. Xenophon gives a long conversation, discussing the terms of peace, in the course of which Cyrus asked Tigranes, who was newly married and greatly loved his wife, what he would give to regain her freedom, she having fallen into the hands of the victor, together with the other women of the royal family. "Cyrus," was the Prince's reply, "to save her from servitude, I would lay down my life."

On which Cyrus replied: "Take, then, thine own, for I cannot reckon that she is properly our captive, for thou didst never flee from us." Then, turning to the king, he added: "And thou, Armenian, take thy wife and children, without paying anything for them, that they may know they come to thee freely."

On the return of the king and prince, after this interview, there was much talk at the Armenian court about Cyrus; one spoke of his wisdom, another of his patience and resolution, another of his mildness; one also spoke of his beauty, his fine figure and lofty stature, whereupon Tigranes turned to his wife, saying: "Dost thou think Cyrus handsome?"

"Indeed," she answered, "I never looked at him." "At whom, then, didst thou look?" asked Tigranes. "At him," was the reply, "who said that, to save me from servitude, he would give his own life."

Of all the epics from which Moses of Khorene has derived incidents or of which he gives fragments, the only one that has survived among the people in complete form, with numerous variants, is Sasmadzrer. There is a reference in the Bible to the story which is related in this poem.

In 2 Kings xix. 37, and Isaiah xxxvii. 38, we read:—

"And it came to pass, as he (Sennacherib) was worshipping in the house of Nisroch his god, that Adramelech and Sharezer, his sons, smote him with the sword; and they escaped into the land of Armenia."

Moses of Khorene tells the same story, adding that the Armenian king assigned an abode to Sharezer in the south of Armenia and to Adramelech in the south-east.

The epic, referred to above, relates the doings of the two brothers and their descendants in Armenia, among the rest the founding by them of the city of Sassoon.

The poem is divided into four parts. It is still transmitted orally, word for word, in Armenia; in many places in poetical form. During the last forty years, several versions of it have been taken down in writing and published, and these have received much attention from scholars. We cannot do more than mention this most interesting production; the space at our disposal forbids our giving even an outline of its contents.

So far we have derived our information from the prose versions of passages in the epics found in Moses of Khorene either as quotations or as paraphrased in his own words. But that historian has also given a few extracts from the poems in their original form, being the first historian to do so. To these extracts we now turn.

Although they are very few, they convey some idea of ancient Armenian poetry. The historian says he has himself heard these poems sung to the accompaniment of various musical instruments, of which he gives long and minute descriptions. According to him, these poems were sung chiefly in the province of Goghtan (the present Agulis, in Russian Armenia). This place abounded in gardens and vineyards, and produced a variety of good wines. The people were gay and fond of merry-making. Their love of the old pagan religion and manners still continued long after their conversion to Christianity. In this respect they resembled the Saxons of Germany, and, even in the early part of the fifth century, they observed pagan rites, sometimes openly, sometimes secretly. One of the old Armenian songs, describing the birth of the Armenian king Vahagn, is given in this volume, page 14. This is supposed to be a myth describing the rise of the sun over the sea.

At sunrise the sky gradually becomes light; between the light and the darkness there is a kind of struggle; all nature is waiting in expectancy of a life-giving power, of the rising of the sun. It seems to be this expectancy of nature and man that the poet likens to the travail of heaven, earth, and sea. The "crimson reed" is perhaps the long red gleam sent forth from the East over the sea at dawn.

We have already referred to Vahagn when dealing with Armenian mythology. In, the Armenian translation of the Bible, in 2 Maccabees iv. 19, the name "Vahagn" is substituted for

"Hercules." This name is derived from the Sanscrit words vah, "to bring," and agn, "fire," and therefore means "fire-bringer." In connection with this, it is interesting to compare the Armenian legend with a similar legend in the Rig-Veda. The word "Agni" is the same as "Agn." The god Agni was born of the rising sun, to the accompaniment of thunder and lightning; of Vahagn the song says: "Out of the flame sprang the child." "His hair was of fire and a beard had he of flame"; Agni had "flaming hair and a golden beard." A comparison of the two poems shows that the similarity between them arises, not from the imitation of one poet by the other, but from identity of theme, for the belief in a fire-god or fire-hero, is common to all mythologies. According to Agathangelos, Vahagn was a favorite deity, and his temple at Taron was famous. King Tiridates, when greeting the Armenian people in a manifesto, says: "May Vahagn, of all Armenia, send you courage!" He puts the name of Vahagn after the names of Aramazd and Anahit. But, in Moses of Khorene, Vahagn is little more than an ordinary king, the son of Tigranes I., though the historian gives the story of his birth and his fights with dragons, as related by the poets. He also calls Vahagn the first of the Vahuni or priestly caste; but this caste was far more ancient than the historian thinks, as sun worship is one of the oldest forms of religion.

Moses of Khorene says, moreover, that there was an image of Vahagn in Georgia, where he was worshipped as a god.

As to the form of this poem—we note the parallelism, similar to that of the old Hebrew songs: "To Sisera a prey of diverse colors, a prey of diverse colors of needlework, of diverse colors of needlework, on both sides " (Judges v. 30). [25]

---

[25]   The following lines from a Chaldean description of *Ut-napisti*, the Chaldean Noah's sacrifice after the Flood, furnish an example from Assyrian poetry:--

> "The gods smelled a savor,
> The gods smelled a sweet savor,
> The gods gathered like flies over the sacrifice."

The Song of Deborah, from which we have just quoted, is supposed to be the oldest passage in the Bible, and is a good specimen of ancient oriental poetry.

The songs quoted in Moses of Khorene are also examples of this poetry, and will therefore be welcome to scholars, as throwing light on this class of ancient literature.

The ancient Armenian form of verse has, doubtless, its own national peculiarities. One of its characteristics is that it consists of one main idea expressed in two or more sentences, regularly connected with one another. There are no complex sentences, only short simple ones, and the manner of expression is direct and definite, but, in order that they may not tire the ear by monotony, they are, by means of parallelism, systematically interwoven so as to form one consistent whole. Thus the different sentences become related to one leading thought. The words are carefully chosen and harmonious to the ear. Metaphor and allegory abound. In color and splendor these songs might vie with any classical poem, and their existence is a proof that long before the Christian era the Armenians had a perfected poetical language, which, in its construction, imaginative force, brilliancy, and grammatical development, bears the impress of literary culture.

Most of the nouns and adjectives in this poem are in the diminutive form, which expresses endearment:

karmrik = reddish
egheknik = little reed
patanekik = little boy
achkunk = little eyes
aregakunk = little sun

The adjectives used here do not qualify the nouns, but simply serve as epithets, or attributes, like the adjectives in the Homeric poems. The Armenian word dzirani, [26] used in this poem, does

---

[26] *Dziran* in Armenian means "apricot," therefore *dzirani* ="of apricot color."

not always mean "red"; applied to a robe it means "red," applied to a belt it means "variegated"; it may originally have had the sense of "pleasing" (cf. Russian krasni, which originally meant "beautiful," but now denotes only "red-colored").

Another of these extant songs, belonging to the time before the Christian era, has, as its theme, the love story of King Artashes II., one of the greatest kings of the Arsacid dynasty. The former, as well as all the other stories we have mentioned, belong to the Haikazian dynasty, but the story of Artashes II. belongs to the Arsacid dynasty and is contained in the second book of Moses of Khorene, the contents of which are less legendary than those of the first book. When narrating the story of Artashes, the historian addresses himself to Sahak Bagratuni, by whose command his history was written, in these terms:—

"The doings of Artashes are known to thee, through the epical songs which are sung in the province of Goghtan; that is to say, his founding of Artaxata (Artashat), [27] his alliance by marriage with the royal house of the Alans, his sons and their descendants, the loves of Satenik with the Vishapazuns (progeny of dragons) who were of the race of Astyages; his wars with them, the overthrow of their dynasty, their slaughter, the burning of their palaces, the rivalries of the sons of Artashes, the intrigues of their wives, which further fomented the discord amongst them. Although these things are well known to thee through the epical songs, I will, nevertheless, narrate them again and will explain their allegorical meaning."

Then Moses of Khorene gives, in detail, a prose account of the deeds of Artashes and his son Artavazd, as they are related in the epic of Artashes, quoting, in the course of his narrative, the songs given in this volume on pages 51 and 52.

---

[27] Strabo says about Artaxata that it was built upon a design which Hannibal gave to King Artaxes (Artashes), who made it the capital of Armenia, and Tournefort, the famous French botanist, who traveled in Armenia in the seventeenth century, exclaims, in reference to this fact: "Who could have imagined that Hannibal would come from Africa to Armenia to be engineer to an Armenian king? But so it is."

Besides these songs, there are included in the history two or three metrical lines, which must be extracts from the epic. One of these lines contains the reply of the Alan king when he is asked to give his daughter in marriage to Artashes: "From whence shall brave . . ." (see page 51-52, the last lines, in this volume). The same poem contains a description of the wedding (see page 52 of this volume).

We learn from ancient Armenian historians that weddings were times of great festivity, especially royal weddings. All the people of the country, old and young, were astir. In the great square they danced and sang, hand in hand. There was a special kind of song sung on these occasions, called "Tzutzk."

The marriage of Satenik was unhappy, because, besides the Vishapazuns, she loved Argavan, the chief of the Median prisoners, who was greatly honored by Artashes. Another of the verses quoted by Moses of Khorene refers to this amour of Satenik. These lines throw some light on the nature of ancient Armenian metre. We quote the text here:—

> "Tencha Satenik tenchans
> Zartakhoir khavart
> Ev ztitz khavardzi
> I bardzitzn Argavana."

The sense of the passage is not very clear, as it contains two words the signification of which is disputed. M. Emin holds that the meaning of these two words is the same, both signifying "crown," and he interprets the line as saying that Satenik loves Argavan so dearly that she would gladly exchange her royal crown for his princely diadem. After much controversy among scholars, Professor Khalatian discovered that, in one Armenian dialect, these words are the names of certain plants, about which there was a superstition that, if they were put under the pillow of the beloved being, and afterwards under the pillow of the lover, mutual affection would be ensured; therefore, according to Professor Khalatian, the passage means that Satenik was desirous of getting these plants from under Argavan's pillow.

In the time of Artashes science and poetry flourished.

One of the sons of this king, Vroir, was a poet; another was Artavazd, who was disliked by the people. The poem says that, when the prince was born, the Vishapazuns stole him, and substituted a devil in his place, and it was this evil spirit that went by the name of Prince Artavazd.

In this poem, also, there is an account of the obsequies of Artashes, which were celebrated with great splendor, for he was dearly beloved by his subjects, many of whom committed suicide at his grave, not caring to survive him. His son Artavazd, who was present, became very jealous and uttered a complaint which Moses of Khorene gives in the words of the epic (see page 65 of this volume).

We have omitted many other incidents of the story of Artashes, as given by Moses of Khorene, but it may be gathered, from what we have of the Artashes epic, that the whole poem was very lengthy.

From other sources we know that the poem was sung by minstrels as late as the eleventh century, for the well-known scholar of that time, Grigor Magistros, says in one of his writings that he has heard it, and he quotes some of its lines in their original form.

Artashes died in a foreign country while engaged in a campaign. In his last moments he is seized with home-sickness, as he remembers his fatherland. He recalls the spring of life and of the year, when the light of dewy morn, like a thin mist, is spreading over the towns and villages. The poem gives his dying words:—

> "Who will give me the smoke of the chimneys and the
> morn of Navasard, [28]
> The running of the stag and the coursing of the deer?
> We sounded the horn and beat the drum
> As is the manner of kings."

---

[28] April, when the New Year commenced.

We have already said that Artashes was a popular king, much beloved by his people, whose death was greatly lamented; this being so, no doubt the Artashes epic must have contained some striking dirges, composed in honor of this monarch, but unfortunately neither Moses of Khorene nor Grigor Magistros records any such songs in connection with him. The despair and melancholy which cast their shadow over pagans is conspicuous in ancient Armenian funeral songs. There were companies of professional mourners, called egheramark ("mothers of lamentation"), also there were groups of singing maidens. All these followed the corpse, dressed in black, with disheveled hair, solemnly clapping their hands and moving in a slow dance. Moses of Khorene gives details of such obsequies as we have mentioned. Even now in some parts of Armenia such companies of mourners exist. Faustus Byzand describes minutely the funeral of a prince and gives also an account of the funeral of Queen Tigranuhi, of whom we have already spoken, adding that the songs sung in her praise, on this occasion, were such that Tigranes felt that they uttered all that was passing in his own mind.

The subjects of funeral songs were the life of the deceased, his stature, the manner of his death, and his domestic relations, so that a collection of these songs would furnish a biography.

We have also details of these dirges from other sources. The song opens with a prologue, addressing the deceased and calling on him to arise from his slumbers and carry on his usual occupations. It then goes on to rebuke him for being deaf to the prayers of the survivors and vouchsafing neither word nor smile. Next comes a description of the new dwelling that the departed has chosen for himself; the grave—an abode without doors or windows. Then comes a repetition of the words spoken by the dead man during his last illness, followed by a series of laudatory epithets, and finally there is the recognition that all prayers for his recovery have been unanswered, followed by an epilogue, taking farewell of the deceased and sending messages by him to dead relatives and friends.

We learn from Moses of Khorene that, in his time, besides the epics, there was other pre-Christian Armenian literature, written and unwritten, of various kinds. We have had examples of songs and epical stories in their gradual development from the stage when man was weak and ignorant, when the people sought after the supernatural and the marvelous, and the subject of epic songs was the mystic relation between nature and man, to the stage when the heroes are no longer gods, but men endowed with valor and every other virtue, without spot or flaw. The stories we have described are sufficient to prove that Armenia had a large store of epic and heroic poems, of which unhappily only fragments have come down to us.

Some specimens of other branches of pre-Christian literature figuring in the list of Moses of Khorene are Temple Books and Histories of Temples. Throughout ancient times members of the priestly class were the chroniclers of the nation's history and its instructors in wisdom; and there is no doubt that this was the case in Armenia. We know that the famous Gnosticos Bardazan, in the second century A.D., came to Armenia to collect material for his history, and in the fortress of Ani he made extracts from the Temple History, which was a chronicle of the doings of the Armenian kings.

Armenia had its own written histories which were, for the most part, destroyed on the introduction of Christianity in the fourth century A.D. Moses of Khorene mentions an Armenian historian named Ughup, who was a priest presiding over the temple of Ani in 150 B.C.

To continue the list—we find Books of the Kings, containing chronicles of kings and their works, and Collections of Historical Songs, which were kept in the temples. These collections were in existence in the fifth century A.D. Moses of Khorene gives extracts from them and they were also sung by minstrels.

Tueliatz Songs recounted the doings of kings and princes in chronological order, hence their name, Tueliatz, or chronicles.

There were also other species of literature, such as Historical Legends, not included in the list, from which Moses of Khorene

141

makes quotations elsewhere, such as the History of the Origin of the Bagratuni Race, the History of Haik, and four other books, without titles, of which he speaks with great admiration.

There is mention of a poet, by name David, who wrote The Wars between Armenia and Media, founding his narrative on Armenian minstrel songs. Unfortunately, none of his works have come down to us.

There is also mention of an Armenian translation, from the Greek, of an epic called Legends of Aramasdes and Hermia. Some scholars think that this must be one of the lost books of Homer, as there are still extant some fragments of an Armenian translation of the Homeric poems.

The Hindus believed that originally dramas were invented by the gods and were performed in heaven. They were brought to earth by Brahma and introduced to men. Whether the ancient Armenians held a similar belief we cannot tell, but it appears that they had, in early times, a drama of their own. The themes of their plays were the doings of the gods of the earth, but there is no record that in Armenia drama ever reached such a high level as it attained in Greece. It may be noticed that, though Persia, the neighbor of Armenia, was rich in lyric and epic poetry, it produced no dramatic literature. It is true that, in Mohammedan times, the Persians had a religious drama; but this merely formed part of their worship and has never had an independent development.

But the Armenians must have done better, as mention is made of Armenian drama by Greek and Roman writers, from whom we learn that King Artavazd I. [29] wrote tragedies, some of which were known to Plutarch. We also learn from Plutarch and others that, in the time of Tigranes II., there were theatres in Armenia, and Plutarch records that, when Lucullus entered Tigranocerta, he found a body of actors busily engaged in preparing to produce a drama in the theatre newly built by Tigranes, and made use of them in the games and other public diversions in honor of his

---

[29] The son of Tigran the Great.

victory. Armenian historians also make mention of the theatres in Armenia. As late as the fifth century A.D., Hovhannes Mandakuni, a religious author, wrote an essay against theatres and actors, which shows that, even after the introduction of Christianity, drama survived in Armenia.

At later periods, in Law Books, restrictions on theatres are mentioned.

In order to determine the date of the Heroic Poems, we must define the different periods of Armenian history. It is now generally accepted by scholars that, towards the end of the seventh century B.C., the Vannic or Chaldean kingdom fell before the invading hordes of Cimmerians or Scythians, and, during the period of anarchy, Armenians also entered the country, which was henceforth to bear the name of "Armenia." The only uncertainty with regard to this migration is about the date. It is universally agreed that it cannot have been later than the seventh century B.C., though it may have been earlier. In the fifth century B.C. Xenophon found Armenia an established kingdom under Tigranes I. Vahe was the last of the Haikazian dynasty. He fell in the war with Alexander the Great in 330 B.C.

The next Armenian dynasty was that of the Arsacidae, of which the first king was Wagharshag I., whose reign began in 149 B.C.

All the epical songs that we have mentioned belong to the Haikazian period, except the Artashes Cycle, which belongs to the Arsacid period. During the 185 years between these two periods, there was no national independence to supply themes for new epics and therefore there is no heroic poetry belonging to this interval.

The second period of Armenian literature (before the establishment of Christianity) extends from the accession of the Arsacid dynasty to the fourth century A.D.

During this period, learning flourished and the libraries in the temples and palaces were the centre of culture. The libraries in palaces were open to any one who wished to consult the archives with a view to writing histories of the countries, and in the temples the priests were engaged in compiling records of the past. In these libraries the histories of the Haikazian dynasty were kept. To this period belongs the epic of Artashes.

Under the rule of the Arsacidae, the number of the nobles greatly increased and the chief amusement of the king and the nobility was sport. Nearly every noble had his own park, which was full of all kinds of deer and in which special sporting parties were given. One of the chief attractions of these parties was the minstrels who sang songs specially composed for the occasion. As upwards of seventy families were ennobled under the Arsacidae, and entertainments were given both by them and by those of lower rank, it will be understood that the number of minstrels must have been large.

As we have mentioned, to this period belongs the Artashes Cycle (A.D. 85-126).

We have also some evidence as to the date of the epics from foreign sources. Armenian epics must have been known, not only in Armenia itself, but in other countries. In migration, their form must sometimes have changed, as, in Plato, we have found the legend of Ara transformed into the story of Er. As the story of Ara was known to Plato, we may take for granted that it existed in the fourth century B.C.

Strabo gives an erroneous etymology of the name "Armenia," which he derives from "Armenios." [30] Perhaps he had heard of Aram, whose story is told in the epics. This story is known to us through Moses of Khorene, who derives the word "Armenia" from Aram, and says that the country was called by this name only by foreigners. As to the etymology of the word "Armenia," there are many different opinions which we cannot discuss here; we will only say that the name "Armenia" is found in an inscription of Darius Hystaspes (510 B.C.).

---

[30] "Armenios, one of the Argonauts, who was believed to have been a native of Rhodes or of Armenion in Thessaly, and to have settled in the country which was called after him, *Armenia*" (Strabo, xi. 530, etc.; Justin, xlii. 2; Steph. Byz. S. V. Αρμενια).

We confine ourselves to one more foreign reference to Armenian epics, viz., that of the philosopher Olympiodorus, who, in an assembly of wise men at Athens, gave an account of an old book which had existed in former times and which contained the history of Noah and his descendants. He added that the incidents related in this book were still sung by Armenian minstrels to the accompaniment of various musical instruments.

Moses of Khorene

We have frequently quoted Moses of Khorene, whose work contains all the extant remains of the epics and all the information that has come down to us with regard to these poems. In fact the first book of his History, as well as the first nine chapters of Book II., consists of summaries and quotations from epics, together with other legends. In taking leave of the pre-Christian period of Armenia let us cast a glance on this historian and his work.

Moses of Khorene was born some time between A.D. 404 and 408. He was one of those young Armenians who were sent by the ecclesiastical authorities to Greece for higher education. After completing his studies, he worked in the libraries of Alexandria, Palestine, and other places. On his return from Palestine, he was shipwrecked on the coast of Italy; thence he went to Rome, Athens, and Byzantium, returning to Armenia about 440. He found his benefactors dead, the Arsacid dynasty extinct, and Christianity endangered by the Persians. It is said that on his return he was so disappointed in both the clergy and the laity— being especially grieved by the ignorance of the former—that he retired into solitude and remained concealed for some time. It happened that the Catholicos Gute, while traveling, alighted at a certain village where he was entertained by the peasants, each of whom made a short speech in his honor. An old man who was of the company was urged also to say something. At first he excused himself on the plea that he was a stranger, but, on being further pressed, to the surprise of all present, he recited an impromptu ode greeting the Catholicos and ended by disclosing his identity, proclaiming himself Moses of Khorene. At first the Catholicos was incredulous, but, on a careful examination of the old man's features, he recognized him as one of his former fellow-students, whereupon he burst into tears and held him in a long embrace.

That day was one of great rejoicing in Armenia, and, soon after, Moses became Bishop of Bagravand.

These Armenian students educated abroad were looked on askance by some of the ignorant clergy, and, for this reason, some of the former used to retire and study in seclusion. In his History, Moses of Khorene inveighs bitterly against these illiterate priests.

Ghazar Pharpe says:—

"Moses, the philosopher of blessed memory, met with much opposition and annoyance from the unlearned clergy, who called this enlightened man a heretic, and in their ignorance found fault with his books, besides performing many unfriendly acts towards him."

After this passage, several pages of the manuscript are missing. The next page we have begins:—

"They exhumed his bones from the grave and threw them into the river."

It is doubtful whether these words refer to Moses or to some one else.

Moses of Khorene attempted to write the history of two or three thousand years, beginning with dark and unknown ages, weaving his materials in such a way as to produce a vivid and life-like picture, tinged with the colors of all the centuries which he depicts. He writes in poetic language and his style is simple and picturesque. Every event recorded by him becomes beautiful, noble, and great. There is not a paragraph, not a sentence, which falls below the general level of the work. The History is a marvelous panorama, which, as it unfolds, fills us with ever fresh wonder and admiration. The story of Tiridates is narrated in such a way as to draw tears from every reader and—to use an Armenian expression—to make him feel as if the hairs of his head had turned into thorns. He speaks with such warm admiration of Tigranes that it might be thought he was speaking of a contemporary.

In the following passage he displays strong feeling, in reference to one of his teachers whom he found dead on his return from abroad.

"Where is the calm of those gentle eyes, which to the just gave rest, and inspired the guilty with awe?

"Where is the smile of his cheerful lips, as he met his pupils?

"Where is the hope that enlivened the tedium of weary journeys? that gave repose in the midst of labor?

"How shall I write my tragedy? and who is there to weep at it?"

One sees by his writing that Moses was a man of strong character, with firm principles, neither vacillating nor superficial. The reader is profoundly impressed by his words; they sink deeply into him, pressing like lead on a tablet, and casting him under the spell of the author. This effect is due, in part, to his convincing power; it is impossible not to realize what he records. His statements are concise; what others would take pages to express, he conveys in a few words. In descriptive powers he is unrivalled, not only among Armenians, but even as compared with Greek and Roman historians. His graphic pictures of people and places, together with his remarks and reflections and his frequent quotations from the national epics, prove his historical skill and literary taste.

In a word, as one reads him, one feels him to be a genius of the first magnitude.

Moses of Khorene wrote his History at the request of Sahak Bagratuni, a man of noble or princely birth. The History consists of three books. Book I., as we have already said, is mainly based on national epics and legends. Although these relate only to a few heroes, the treatment is very elaborate.

Then comes the history of 180 years, over which he passes very lightly, merely giving a list of names, with a few words added to each. This shows that, for this period, he has not been able to find any material in the native epics and songs.

Book II. relates to the Arsacid dynasty, speaking also of the introduction of Christianity, and going on to the death of Tiridates and of Gregory the Illuminator.

Book III. contains the history of the successors of Tiridates up to the sad end of the Arsacid dynasty. This book ends with a long lament over the pitiful plight of Armenia. It contains also a bitter invective against the author's contemporaries—princes, judges, clergy, soldiery—in short against all who, being careless of duty and regardless of the ideal, lead the people astray.

Moses of Khorene has left other works besides his History, one of which is a Geography, containing, among other things, an account of the British Isles.

For 1400 years, the History of Moses of Khorene was revered and accepted as the only authentic History of Armenia; and it was not till the nineteenth century that criticism was directed against it, not only by Armenian scholars, but also by French, German, Italian, English, and Russian scholars. This criticism was chiefly leveled at the principal source from which the Armenian historian professed to draw his information.

Arshak the Great, according to Moses, after casting off the Macedonian yoke and conquering Assyria, set his brother, Wargharshak, on the throne of Armenia. So commences the Arsacid dynasty. The new king wished to know what kind of men had been ruling the country before him. Was he (he asked) the successor of brave men or of bad men He found an intelligent man, a Syrian, named Mar-Abas-Katina, and sent him to his brother, Arshak the Great, with this letter:—

"To Arshak, the king of the earth and the sea, whose form and person are like unto the gods and whose triumphs are above those of all kings; the greatness of whose mind can fathom all things of earth, Wargharshak, thy youngest brother and comrade in arms, appointed by thee King of Armenia, greeting, Victory ever attend thee.

"I have received from thee the behest to encourage bravery and wisdom. I have not forgotten thy counsel. On the contrary, I have done all that my mind could devise or my skill carry into effect, and now, thanks to thy guardianship, I have put this country in order. And next I want to know who, before myself, has subdued the land of Armenia, and from whom are descended the noble families who are established here. There does not seem to be any fixed grade of classes; among the chief men, it is impossible to ascertain which is highest and which lowest; so that some confusion ensues. I therefore beg that the archives may be opened in the presence of this man whom I have sent to present himself in thy great country, in order that he may bring back the information that is desired by thy son and brother."

This Syrian (says the historian) found in the library at Nineveh a book translated from the Chaldean into Greek, by order of Alexander the Great, which contained various ancient histories. From this book Mar-Abas copied only the authentic history of Armenia, which he took back to Wargharshak, who, esteeming this document his most precious treasure, preserved it with great care in his palace and engraved part of it on a stone monument.

It is this document of Mar-Abas-Katina that Moses of Khorene cites as his chief authority for the early authentic history of Armenia, though he also mentions several other native and foreign writers as sources of his work.

With regard to these statements, critics point out that the library of Nineveh was not in existence in the second century B.C., as it was destroyed in 625 B.C.; some even maintain that Mar-Abas-Katina was a fictitious personage, invented by Moses of Khorene to give more weight to his own statements, in accordance with the universal custom of his time, when contemporary writings were continually ascribed to the great men of old or even to imaginary characters. Moses of Khorene, say these critics, was himself a great lover of the folklore, legends, and epics of his country, but he knew that, if he gave these as his only source of information, his History would gain no credence, especially as, at the period when he wrote, just after the establishment of Christianity, everything pagan was regarded with suspicion. Moreover, Moses, being himself a bishop, could not have avowed such a source for all his statements, though, as we have said, he quotes from the epics and says that some of the contents of his work are derived from them. It is, however, generally admitted that Moses of Khorene had in his hands such a book as he describes and that this book was one of his sources. The book has even been traced.

As to Mar-Abas-Katina, although his book may not have been compiled under the circumstances described in the History, Moses may have believed that he was the author of the book in his possession. Professor Mar has even found, in Arabic literature, some independent traces of Mar-Abas-Katina.

There is also some controversy about the date of Moses of Khorene himself. By some he is placed even as late as the seventh century, because his writings contain references to events as late as that period.

But it is not difficult to account for this without disputing the generally received date of the historian, for, when we consider how many ancient books have been re-edited, we see how easily the work before us may have been touched up by a later hand in the seventh century. [31]

In concluding this account of Moses of Khorene, we must acknowledge that he has not only rendered much service to Armenian history, but that his book is one of the great works of

---

[31] Translations of Moses of Khorene: *Latin* (with Armenian text), Whiston (G. & G.), *London*, 1736; *Italian*, Cappelletti (G.), Venice, 1841; Tommaseo (H.), Venice, 1849-50; *German*, Lauer (M.), Regensburg, 1869; *French* (with Armenian text), Le Vaillant de Florivel (P. E.), Paris, 1841 (2 vols.), and in Langlois' Collection, vol. ii.; *Russian*, M. Emin, Moscow.

all literature, and, if it were better known, would take a high place among the masterpieces of the world.

Adoption of Christianity

The most momentous event in the national life of Armenia—an event which was the chief determining factor in the early history of the country—was the change of religion made by the adoption of Christianity, the foundation of which had been already laid by King Abgarus (A.D. 3-34) and the preaching of the Apostles St. Thaddeus (A.D. 33-48) and St. Bartholomew (A.D. 49), and finally established by Tiridates (A.D. 286-342). By this the Armenians were entirely severed from the pagan Persians and brought into close contact with the Greeks, whose representative was then the Emperor of Byzantium. As a result of this religious agreement, a treaty was concluded in 319 between Tiridates and Constantine, the first Christian Emperor of Rome, by which the two Christian monarchs bound themselves to defend each other against all pagans.

The adoption of Christianity meant, to the Armenians, a revolution in their whole view of life, a severance from their ancestral beliefs, though these beliefs have left traces in Armenian folklore which are visible even to this day. These beliefs and the folklore arising out of them were regarded by the Christian clergy as a poisonous flower grown up in the fields of paganism. The historians of the period have chronicled the efforts of the clergy to exterminate every relic of the old faith. Temples were pulled down and churches built in their stead; images and other monuments were broken in pieces; heathen books and records were destroyed; pagan festivals were turned into Christian ones. We learn from Faustus of Byzantium that laws were even made against the use and the singing of pagan songs, but, notwithstanding this persecution, according to Faustus and other historians, the Armenians "languished for these songs." Even as late as the fifth century, when there was an attempt to restore paganism in Armenia, Vasak Suni had books of these songs copied and distributed among the people in order to win them back to heathenism. This had the effect of rekindling hostility against the songs, and the books were destroyed when Christianity finally triumphed, although, as we have shown above, echoes of the songs are to be heard as late as the eleventh century.

Gregory the Illuminator (A.D. 239-325), who converted Armenia to Christianity, belonged to the royal race of the Arsacidae. He had studied at Caesarea. He and his family had Hellenizing tendencies in religion, education, and politics. There was a section opposed to Hellenism which favored Syrian ideas and, in politics, inclined to Persia. At this early period of Christianity, the Bible was read in Greek in the north-west provinces of Armenia, while in the south-east provinces it was read in Syriac. During this period, schools were established for the education of the young on Christian principles. Out of the pupils in these schools about 100 were chosen to be sent to educational centers abroad, where Greek learning was taught. At the time when this contact of Armenians with Greek culture took place, the ancient glories of Hellas were past, and Greek scholars busied themselves chiefly with theological subtilties. Of course the main object of educating the students from the Christian schools was to indoctrinate them in religious lore and fit them for the priesthood, but, nevertheless, the youths also brought away with them a tincture of Greek culture, and this led to the rise of the Golden Age of Armenian literature.

It was the aim of the Greek Empire at this time to make the Armenian Church a branch of the Greek Church and to gain a political ascendancy over the Armenians, but the head of the Armenian Church and the leaders of the intellectual movement were resolved on religious and national independence. Towards that end two important steps were taken. In 404, the Armenian alphabet was invented, and, in 491, the Armenian Church was separated from the Greek Church.

The Armenian language belongs to the Indo-European group. Though it has been regarded by some as an offshoot of the Iranic branch, recent scholars of eminence have maintained its right to rank as a distinct branch, intermediate between the Iranic and the European. It has a very independent character and many peculiarities of its own; it has also great strength and flexibility. It has a great number of roots, and is capable of expressing ideas of all kinds and denoting fine shades of meaning. It is read from left to right like European languages. It is rich in particles, to which circumstance its expressiveness is partly due. It has also a treasure of dialectic words, which have the effect of importing vigor to Armenian speech. It is not harsh in sound, as has been alleged by some who are imperfectly acquainted with it. Its alphabet consists of thirty-six characters, with which it is possible to represent every variety of sound, consisting of vowels as well as consonants; it has no vowel points, in this respect resembling the European, and differing from most oriental, alphabets. The spelling is almost perfectly phonetic.

The language of the period with which we are dealing was Grabar or Ancient Armenian, which remained the literary language till the beginning of the nineteenth century and is still the Church language, being used in all religious services. Modern Armenian has not departed very widely from Grabar. During pagan times, the Armenians had an alphabet of their own, but, on the introduction of Christianity, it was discarded on account of its pagan origin.

The honor of being the inventor of the new Armenian alphabet belongs to St. Mesrop (361-440), a former secretary of King Tiridates. He found some of the ancient letters and invented others to complete the alphabet in 404. St. Mesrop and St. Sahak (353-439) were the forerunners of the Armenian intellectual movement, the former as the inventor of the alphabet, the latter, together with his pupils, as the translator of the Bible into Armenian. This translation is called "the Queen of Translations." The language is so simple and direct, and, at the same time, so beautiful, that there is nothing to be compared with it.

The Armenian translation of the Bible is the foundation-stone of Armenian Christianity. Perhaps no translation of the Scriptures has ever made so deep an impression on a people as this one has made on the Armenians. By them it was taken as a symbolical history of their own country. Did not the events recorded in the very first chapters happen in Armenia? and also the second Creation after the Flood? Did not their beloved mountain, Ararat, figure in the latter story? In the Bible they found even the names of their national heroes, Haik and Vahagn, though, as we have seen, for the latter names only the translators are responsible. Other Bible stories resemble the records of Armenian history. Moses led his tribe from the land of bondage into a land of freedom, just as Haik did. All the stories of suffering under a foreign yoke and of revolt against oppression have their parallels in the annals of Armenia.

Golden Age of Armenian Literature

At the end of the fourth century (374-383), Nerses the Great was Catholicos. During these ten years he displayed great energy. Under his rule, many councils were held and many regulations drawn up to safeguard the morals of the people. In addition to this, a number of schools, hospitals, orphanages, almshouses, and other charitable institutions arose under his supervision. A contemporary historian says that during Nerses' term of office, upwards of 2000 abbeys and monasteries were built. These religious houses served as centers, not only of religious life, but also of learning, where numerous ecclesiastics and teachers were trained. This intellectual movement, which was of a purely religious and educational character, not merely lived through the political tempest of those times, but gradually grew and progressed. In the year 400, the representative of the Arsacid dynasty on the throne was Vramshapuh, an able monarch, who, being himself a lover of peace, did much to encourage and foster the intellectual movement and to keep the country free from foreign foes and internal dissensions. King Vramshapuh reigned twenty-one years and it was, approximately, these years that constituted what is called "the Golden Age of Armenian literature."

St. Sahak (353-439), who, with St. Mesrop, was the moving spirit of the intellectual movement, was Catholicos during part of this period.

The Golden Period was of short duration, only lasting twenty-five years, but it was rich in achievements. The students educated abroad on their return originated a new literature, pervaded by Christian ideas. They considered themselves as torch-bearers in the new movement, and all their work is animated by inspiration.

This period is one of marvelous activity. The new national alphabet had charms that wrought like magic and, coupled with the new religion of hope, captivated all Armenian hearts. Armenians realized that it was a religion for the people, not merely for the great and powerful. All over Armenia national schools were opened. Nearly every book of importance written in Greek and Syriac was translated into Armenian, as well as some of the Latin authors. Translation was a recognized profession, and "translator" was a title of honor, like the European "doctor." There are upwards of fifty chronicles and histories written in ancient Armenian, which is richer in literature than the Greek of the same period, and the Armenian language is so flexible and so well adapted to the exact rendering of every kind of literature that if, for instance, the Anabasis of Xenophon were lost, it might be reproduced in Greek, almost word for word, from the Armenian version. Among the writings which now survive only in Armenian, the originals having been lost, are the Homilies of St. John Chrysostom, two works of Philo on Providence, together with some of his Biblical commentaries, the Chronicle of Eusebius, the works of St. Ephrem and others.

Besides translations, Armenia produced, during the period with which we are concerned, original works, chiefly of an historical character. These give very succinct accounts of the Persian and Mongol invasions, and throw fresh light on the state of the East during the Middle Ages. As these works lie outside our present subject, we cannot here even name their authors. Those who wish to investigate them are referred to what we have written elsewhere. [32]

What is most remarkable is that, at the very beginning of the intellectual movement, when the alphabet had just been formed, the literary language is so highly developed, so rich and subtle, that it is more like a language which is the product of centuries of culture. This very fact shows that culture was no novelty in Armenia. The new movement only introduced a fresh era in Armenian civilization.

Twenty-five years after the introduction of the Armenian alphabet, the Arsacid dynasty fell (428), the last king being Artashir III. From this time the Armenians have ceased to be politically independent.

From 432 onwards, the greater part of Armenia was governed by Persian satraps. The Persians regarded with great apprehension the adoption of Christianity in Armenia, as this caused the Armenians to enter into closer relations with the Greeks. As a matter of fact, at the end of the fourth century, the Greeks came to aid the Armenians in driving away the Persians. It was the aim of the Persians to eradicate Christianity from Armenia. In order to further this object, they declared war on the Greek Empire. The latter, instead of fighting, made peace with the Persians, accepting very humiliating terms. The Armenians were left to their fate, but, nevertheless, they resolved to stand up for their religion against the Persian monarch, who led a great army against them with the intention of enforcing Zoroastrianism. At this time there was no Armenian king. The majority of the remaining princes and nobles, however, formed a regular army, the people gladly serving as volunteers, though there was a very small party, led by Prince Vasak Suni, that were inclined, for political reasons, to entertain the Persian proposals.

All this took place between 449 and 454. The first religious war (451) is known as Vardanantz, because Vardan Mamikonian, who was the commander-in-chief of the Armenian army of defence,

---

[32] See *Travel and Politics in Armenia*, by Noel Buxton, MP., and Rev. Harold Buxton; with Introduction by Viscount Bryce and *A Contribution on Armenian History and Culture* by Aram Raffi. Smith, Elder & Co. 1914.

was the moving spirit in the struggle of Armenian Christianity against the religion of Persia. He fell in the battle of Avarayr, but his fame survived him and he is the most beloved of Armenian heroes.

This war, though it crushed the hopes in which the Armenians had indulged themselves of regaining their political independence, nevertheless convinced the Persians of the impossibility of uprooting a religion which was so firmly implanted in the hearts of the people.

The first religious war was followed by a second, in which the Armenian princes offered a valiant resistance and the Persians were obliged to give way. The leader of the resisting princes was appointed satrap by the Persians. Thus Armenia won back partial independence, the Persians themselves appointing an Armenian satrap and proclaiming religious liberty. The Chief of the Magi, who was sent to convert the Armenians to Mazdaism, returned unsuccessful and reported to the Persian king: "Even if the immortals themselves came to our aid, it would be impossible to establish Mazdaism in Armenia." Although Vardan and his followers perished in this war, and although the Armenians, apparently, lost the battle, the struggle resulted in the triumph of the ideal for which Armenia was struggling—that of religious freedom. This the Persians realized and never, after this time, did they make any attempt to force the Armenians to change their faith. Neither did any of the various Mohammedan conquerors venture on any steps towards bringing about the conversion of the whole Armenian nation, though they have enforced conformity on a small scale; they have had to content themselves with political supremacy. The Mohammedan world has realized that Christianity is a great power in Armenia, and this is the reason why the religious heads of the nation—the Catholicos and the patriarchs—meet with great consideration, not only from the governments of Christian states, but also from Mohammedan powers; both by Christian and by Mohammedan countries which have rule over Armenia these dignitaries are recognized as representatives of their country, not only in religious, but also in secular affairs. Thus the Christian National Church has been one of the chief factors of the unity and the national consciousness which exists among Armenians even up to the present day, and this is the reason why the battle of Vardan is regarded as a national triumph and is still annually commemorated.

Middle Ages

When Armenia had ceased to be an independent state, its literature became more religious, as the clergy were anxious to foster devotion. Christianity introduced a new kind of poetry, namely, Church hymns and chants. These were called, in Armenian, sharakans. They were not only written in metre, but they were composed with a view to being sung. The word sharakan means a "row of gems." Historians of the Middle Ages say that the sharakans were mainly written by the "translators," i.e., by writers of the fourth and fifth centuries. As a matter of fact, very few sharakans were written after the thirteenth century. Since then, no prayers or hymns have been introduced into the Armenian Church.

It is said by writers of the Middle Ages that St. Sahak arranged the sharakans for ten voices and St. Stephanos for twenty-six voices, corresponding to created things—elements, plants, birds, and animals. There were also women sharakan writers. One of these was Sahakadukht, who lived in the eighth century. She not only wrote, but also composed music, and taught singing. Out of modesty, she used to hide behind a curtain, whence she gave instruction to both sexes. An historian of the time, Ghevond Eretz, says of her sharakans: "They were angelic songs on earth." Singing was considered a great art in Armenia, and musicians were called "philosophers." Several of such "philosophers" were canonised and had the word "philosopher" prefixed to their names. The fame of some of these musicians spread to foreign lands. This explains the fact that, when Catholicos Petros Getadardz went to Constantinople, he took with him a company of musicians, whom he presented, as a gift, for the service of the Byzantine court.

There was a revival of sharakan-writing in the thirteenth century, which was a flourishing literary period. It was during this time that Bishop Khachatour Tarinetzi invented distinctively Armenian musical notes, which are quite unrelated to European ones, so that the Armenians had now, not only an alphabet of their own, but also their own musical notation, and their hymns could be set to music. This notation was improved in the eighteenth century.

Armenian hymns are written in a style which is not only picturesque, but which also has a charm of its own; its colors are very rich; the pictures it conjures up are vivid. When one remembers that many of them were written when national life and death were hanging in the balance, because of foreign oppression, at a time when they had no one to turn to but the Creator, we understand how it is that so much tenderness, hope, and devotion are embodied in these "rows of gems," nor can one help thinking that Armenian is the natural language for religious poems. A vein of mysticism runs through many of these hymns, especially through those written by Gregory of Narek (951-1009), one example of which—"The Christ-Child"—appears on page 106 of this volume. But this mysticism is not obscure; on the contrary, it is to the hymn what light and shade are to a picture serving to bring it into touch with nature.

Hymns have always been popular among the Armenians. Even peasants know them by heart and sing them. The hymn tunes are unique, being entirely independent of those of other Christian nations. Their somewhat strange rhythm recalls the chorus of singers round the altars of the pagan gods. No doubt some pagan melodies have found their way into the Christian hymn tunes of Armenia.

The Armenians are rich in folksongs. The music to which these songs are set possesses great charm. In it, also, the rhythm is most important. An Armenian composer, speaking of these folksongs, says:—

"By means of those ethereal and heavenly waves of melody one sees enchanting mermaids who, after dancing on the banks of large and small lakes and poising themselves on the waters, allure towards themselves the pagan Armenians, offering love kisses to all minstrels."

In later years Armenian music and poetry were affected by European influence, but in her hymns and folksongs she has musical treasures that are all her own.

Side by side with the written literature of this period, the unwritten literature continued to grow. The latter consists mainly of folktales, fables, and proverbs.

It is easy to distinguish a Christian folktale from a pagan one by the different ideals embodied in it. Some of the folktales of this period have arisen out of historical events.

In the folktales, it is the youngest child that is the hero or heroine. These stories express the people's outlook on life and are the product of their experiences, which have been handed down from generation to generation.

There is a great deal of folklore current in Armenia, some of which has been collected and published.

Grigor Magistros says that, in his time, unwritten fables in rhyme were very popular.

There are also many Armenian proverbs. It seems to have been a custom in ancient times —and the usage is still retained in some places—for a man to go and meet the girl he wishes to marry on the banks of a stream or in a forest and to ask her a riddle. If she gives the correct answer to the riddle, he marries her.

Here are a few of the riddles used on these occasions:—

"What paper is it that you cannot write on? and what sort of pen can write on this paper?"

A maiden who desires to marry the man should answer:—

"The heart is the paper on which no pen can write; language is

160

the pen that writes on the heart."

"What rose is it that opens in the winter and in due time fades and is gone?"

Answer: "Snow is the rose that opens in the winter; when summer comes, it fades and is gone."

"The brother chases the sister, the sister the brother, but neither can catch the other."

Answer: "The sun and the moon."

There is another usage, belonging especially to young girls, which has given rise to an extensive literature. This literature consists of charm-verses, which are used for fortune-telling. A selection of these is given on pages 67-68.

Once a year, on the Eve of Ascension Day, young maidens who want their fortunes told decorate a bowl with certain specially selected flowers. Into this bowl each girl casts a token —a ring, a brooch, a thimble. After filling the bowl with flowers of seven different kinds, and water drawn from seven springs, they cover it with an embroidered cloth and take it by night to the priest, who says a prayer over it. They then put it out in the moonlight, open to the stars, leaving it till dawn. Next morning, at daybreak, furnished with provisions for the whole day, they go out of the village carrying the bowl, to the side of a spring, to the foot of a mountain, or into an open field, gathering, on the way, various kinds of flowers, with which they deck themselves. Arrived at their destination, they first play games, dance, and sing, then they take a beautiful little girl, too young to tell where the sun rises, who has been previously chosen for their purpose and gaily dressed for the occasion, and who does not know to whom each token belongs, and cover her face with a richly wrought veil, so that she may not see what is in the bowl. The child draws the articles out of the bowl, one by one, and holds each in her hand. While she does this, one of the party recites a charm-song, and the owner of each token takes the song which accompanies it as her fortune.

There are thousands of these charm-songs. In form they are very simple. Sometimes two consecutive lines deal with quite distinct subjects, though they rhyme together and their construction is the same. Each is a perfect poem.

After the end of the Arsacid dynasty, Armenia remained under the rule of Persia for two hundred years. During this period, sometimes the whole country fell temporarily into the hands of the Greeks; on other occasions the same fate befell a few provinces. Speaking generally, after the fall of the Arsacidae, the eastern—and more extensive—part of Armenia remained under Persian rule, and the western—and smaller—part came under Greek dominion. The Greeks and the Persians were continually fighting with one another for the possession of the whole country. Armenia was the battlefield, and the sufferer was always the Armenian people. After the Arabs had embraced Mohammedanism, they formed a powerful empire, conquering Mesopotamia and then passing on to Persia. They forced the Persians to become Mohammedans, and in 640 entered Armenia. Eastern Armenia, which was then in the hands of the Persians, fell into their possession.

The Greeks greatly dreaded the taking of Armenia by the Arabs, as it formed a strong barrier against the assault of the Greek colonies in Asia Minor. Therefore, as they had before fought in Armenia against the Persians, so they now proceeded to fight against the Arabs; and again Armenia was the battlefield and the sufferers were the Armenians. The Greeks came from time to time demanding tribute of them, and if their demand were resisted, the people were plundered and slaughtered. On the departure of the Greek army, the Arabs came, making the same demand. Thus, during the first two hundred years following the fall of the Arsacidae, the Armenians were between the two fires of the Persians and the Greeks, and then for another two hundred years between the two fires of the Greeks and the Arabs. During this period, the Armenian princes offered resistance from time to time and succeeded in regaining independence for short intervals. The governors set by the Arabs over Armenia were in the habit of persecuting the native princes, to prevent them from organizing revolts. Of these governors, the most bloodthirsty

162

were Kashm and Bugha. The former cunningly invited all the Armenian princes to the town of Nakhejevan, where they assembled in the church; whereupon, by order of the government, the church was surrounded by piles of wood and set on fire, and the princes burnt alive (704). The army was then set to plunder and slaughter the Armenians and burn the towns and villages, as the people, deprived of their princes, could offer no resistance. Many were exiled to the Arab capital, Damascus. Bugha (850) surpassed even Kashm in his cruelty, but we need not chronicle his atrocities here. Under such governors as these, the tribute and the taxes were enormous, and the people became very poor. There were, however, also good governors, during whose rule the people were free from oppression and were allowed to pursue their peaceful occupations.

But gradually the power of the Arabs declined.

Bagratuni Dynasty

The Armenians took advantage of the weakening of the Arab power to form independent kingdoms. One of the principal noble families during the period of Arab dominion was that of the Bagratuni. This family was rich and powerful and had much land in its possession. Under the Arsacidae, the head of this family was hereditary "coronator" (i.e., he had the privilege of putting the crown on the king's head, on the occasion of a new sovereign). During the rule of the Arabs, the command of the Armenian army was given to this family. The Bagratuni, though extremely courageous and patriotic, were also cautious and tactful in their relations with the Arabs, whom they served faithfully, thus gaining the respect of the Khalifs. As they also won the love and esteem of their own countrymen by rebuilding and restoring what the Arabs had destroyed, they were able to act as mediators between the Khalifs and the Armenian people. In wars against the enemies of the Arabs, members of this family had many successes. Once a Persian prince revolted against the Khalif and a Persian army of 80,000 marched into Armenia. The Arabs were too weak to make any resistance, but Ashot Bagratuni with his troops defeated the invaders. After the victory, the Khalif of Bagdad sent a crown to Ashot, thus making him a king, thinking, "He is so powerful that, if I do not give him a crown, he will seize one for himself."

Thus in 885 Ashot became the first king of the Bagratuni dynasty. The Greek emperor, Basil I., also sent a crown to Ashot, with a view to gaining the friendship and influence of Armenia. During the dominion of the Bagratuni, the régime of the Arsacidae was restored and the country prospered. Ani, which was the seat of government during the greater part of this period, though formerly it was little more than a fortress, became one of the most flourishing cities of the time. It was full of fine edifices—churches, palaces, museums, etc.—and was called "the city of a thousand and one churches." Its fame even spread to foreign lands.

There were several other noble Armenian families with ambitions. In 908 one of these—the Ardzruni family—made the lands they held into a kingdom, called Vaspurakan, with Van as a capital city. In taking this step they were encouraged by the Arabs, who were watching with alarm the growing power of the Bagratuni.

In 908 another Armenian kingdom was set up with Kars as its capital.

Ashot III., who was then the king of the Bagratuni dynasty, was quite aware that the Arabs were encouraging the formation of small Armenian kingdoms, but he offered no opposition, leaving his rivals alone to serve the people each in his own way.

This Ashot was one of the greatest sovereigns of this dynasty. He was called "Ashot the Compassionate" because of his love of the people and his numerous charitable provisions for their benefit. It was said that he would never dine without sending for some beggars out of the street to share the meal with him.

The most renowned as well as the wisest and most powerful king of this dynasty was Gagik I. (990-1020), under whom the country enjoyed its period of greatest prosperity.

The danger of the Arabs was past, but now a new peril threatened the East, that of the Seljukian Turks, who came from Central Asia in search of a new country. Persia and Mesopotamia fell before them and they entered Armenia. Several of the Armenian princes offered them stout resistance with some success, but, fearing that this success was only temporary, others transferred themselves and their subjects to more secure parts of the country.

The Seljuks conquered Persia and established a Persian kingdom of their own, but the new Persia was no longer Zoroastrian, but Mohammedan. Armenia again became a battlefield. The Greeks also claimed the city of Ani, and this led to many conflicts in which the Armenians made a brave defense. The town, however, fell through treachery and the Greeks devastated some parts of the country, treating the inhabitants no better than the Arabs and the Seljuks had done. In order to weaken the power of Armenia, they also made attempts to exterminate the native princes and nobles.

About the same time, the Seljuks again invaded Armenia and completed the desolation which the Greeks had begun. They wrought great destruction in Ani.

The last king of the Bagratuni dynasty was unable to re-establish his kingdom and was killed by the Greeks. His two sons and his grandson were poisoned. So ended the race of the Bagratuni whose dynasty had lasted 160 years.

During the rule of this house, the country had a period of rest and the energies of the people were directed to the restoration and development of the country. The ruined monasteries and churches were rebuilt, schools were again established; commerce, arts, and handicrafts throve. This was a particularly flourishing time for the national architecture, which now assumed a new character. Most of the Armenian abbeys and churches were built during this time, and as these places had always been seats of learning, alternative erudition revived, original writing and the transcription of manuscripts going on briskly within the convent walls. The literature of this period is chiefly of a religious character. In it we see traces of Arabic influence—the influence of the eighth century, when Arabic literature was at its zenith. The chief debt of Armenian literature to the Arabs is the introduction of rhyme, which is first found in Armenian verse in the eleventh century.

In dealing with this period, as we are only concerned with Armenian poetry, we must leave unmentioned the historians and other famous prose writers.

The most remarkable Armenian poet under the Bagratuni dynasty was GRIGOR NAREKATZI (951-1009), who has been called the Pindar of Armenia and has also been canonized as a saint. From his pen came elegies, odes, panegyrics, and homilies. His sacred elegies (ninety-five in number) are elevated in style, showing Arabian influence, and very pure in sentiment. His canticles and melodies are still chanted in the Armenian Church. Verbosity is a characteristic of his work; in one passage the word "God" is accompanied by ninety adjectives.

He was greatly loved and revered by the people, but he aroused jealousy in some of his ecclesiastical colleagues. On one occasion, they went to the Catholicos with accusations against him. The Catholicos appointed priests to investigate the case. These priests repaired to the abbey where Grigor Narekatzi was, arriving about dinner time on a Friday. To their surprise they found roast pigeons on the table, and reminded Grigor that it was fast-day, whereupon the latter said, addressing himself to the pigeons: "If that be so, off with you!" and the roasted birds took to themselves wings and flew away. The astonished investigators, without going into the case, turned back and reported the miracle to the Catholicos. Of course this is an extravagant legend, but it shows the high estimation in which Grigor Narekatzi was held by his contemporaries.

The greatest work of this writer and the one on which his fame rests is Narek. It is divided into ninety-five chapters, and is a tragic devotional monologue composed of poetical prayers. Here

166

the author reveals his heart and soul in converse with God. Hope, fear, love, faith, repentance, entreaty, aspiration, breathe as if mingled with tears in fine and noble lines and periods. There is a copious stream of epithets, a flood of rhetoric, an unfailing flow of ideas. With all this wealth of diction, this work is sincere and strikingly original, and gives evidence of the author's high-soaring imagination. He begins with an address to God, in which he represents himself as one of the vilest of creatures, saying that, if all the trees in all the forests of the world were pens and all the seas ink, they would not suffice to write down his sins, but towards even such sinfulness as this the mercy of God is great, and the Creator is so powerful that it will be possible for Him to bleach the sins as white as snow.

This work gives evidence that its author had, on the one hand, great love of God and a firm faith, and on the other hand a vivid imagination and poetic fire. All this he has worded together with great skill.

Narek is a mingling of prose and verse. It begins in prose and then breaks into verse, then again, after continuing to some length, returns to prose, and so on. It was printed for the first time in 1673 at Constantinople; in all thirty editions have been published in different places. It stands by itself, being the only long mystic work in Armenian literature, mysticism being quite alien to the typical Armenian mind. Even the mysticism of Narek and a few other works of the same period has its own peculiarities. It is not so obscure as ordinary mysticism, partaking, rather, of the nature of allegory. Notwithstanding its unusual character, Narek was formerly regarded with veneration little short of that accorded to the Bible itself. Within recent times superstitious people ascribed to it miraculous medical qualities, believing that if certain chapters were read over a patient he would be cured. It was also believed that if any one read certain chapters—forty in number—with concentrated attention, banishing thought of everything else, he would have the power of controlling devils, but this it is said is very difficult and even dangerous, because while the reading is going on, evil spirits come and try to distract the mind of the reader, annoying, terrifying, and even torturing him; if his attention wanders, he may become possessed. All this shows the value and importance that were attached to Narek. At the end of this work, the author states that he finished writing it in the year 1001-2. Gregory of Narek also wrote several songs. Some of his prayers and sharakans are used in the church services. Another great writer of this period was Grigor Magistros (-1058) who produced poetry of some value. He was of princely lineage and, unlike the Armenian authors who were his predecessors or contemporaries, he was a layman. He gained reputation as a linguist, a scholar, and a writer, and was one of the greatest politicians of his time. He received the title of "duke" from the Greek emperors Constantine and Monomachus. Early in life he gave up politics and retired to his estate, where he devoted himself to literary pursuits. He wrote both poetry and prose. His chief poetical work is a long metrical narration (a thousand lines in extent) of the principal events recorded in the Bible, from the Creation to the Resurrection of Christ. The author states that this work was written in three days at the request of a Mohammedan noble who wished to make acquaintance with the Christian Scriptures and who, after reading the poem, became converted to Christianity. Grigor Magistros was almost the first poet to adopt the use of rhyme, introduced into Armenia by the Arabs. In his work Grigor Magistros tells some interesting stories which he has learnt from the peasants. One is the following. The lark, fearing that heaven would fall down, lay on her back, stretching up her feet towards the sky, thinking she would thus prevent the catastrophe. Some laughed at her and said, "With your spindle legs, you want to become a tree, O bird, with a mind capacious as the sea." The lark replied, "I am doing what I can."

The Crusades

At the end of the eleventh century, chronicles and histories were written in ancient Armenian (Grabar), but there was also a language of the people, in which books for popular use, such as collections of medical recipes, began to be written at this period, as well as songs. When the country again lost its independence many migrations took place. It was not only peasants and citizens who migrated; some of the nobles also sought more secure dwelling places in mountainous districts. The majority of these settled in the region of the Taurus Mountains, and there the emigrants multiplied to such an extent that they equaled the Greeks in number. In their new home they built many churches and abbeys, where they educated the boys of the settlement. Soon they established a number of villages and small towns, and the princes set up fortresses. The Byzantine emperors rather encouraged this progress, as they thought that the existence of small buffer-states on their frontier would serve as a barrier against the attacks of Mohammedan countries. One of these princes, Rubin by name, established himself there in 1080. He chose an impregnable stronghold, and the Armenians of the neighborhood came and put themselves under his protection. Other Armenian princes, settled in the surrounding districts, adopted him as their chief. Having concentrated and strengthened his power, he ruled his little realm—which was called, after him, the Rubinian Principality—with great wisdom for fifteen years. He was succeeded by his son, Constantine, in 1095. Constantine extended his dominions by taking some almost impregnable fortresses from the Greeks. During his reign many Europeans began to come, with their armies, to the East. They wore the badge of the cross on their arms, and were therefore called "Crusaders." They cleared Palestine and Syria of Mohammedans and set up new Christian principalities in those countries. The Armenians called these strangers "Latins" because they were all Catholics of the Roman Church. Constantine rendered great services to the Crusaders by furnishing them with guides, providing them with provisions, etc., and the European princes, as an acknowledgment, conferred on him the title of "marquis."

The successors of Constantine extended still further the boundaries of the principality. After gaining possession of the mountains and strongholds, they came to the plains of Cilicia and imposed their rule as far as the sea-coast. At this time the Byzantine Empire was very weak, and the Mohammedan Seljuks and Arabs were not very strong, as they had become divided among themselves and were engaged in strife with one another.

The Crusaders had also formed new Christian principalities in those regions, so that the Rubinians had no fears either of Mohammedans or of any other foe. Precisely one hundred years after the accession of Rubin I., the Armenians possessed the extensive reach of territory between the Taurus Range and the sea, where they had built many fortresses, towns, and even ports.

Leo II. (1185) succeeded in repelling the attacks of the Sultan of Damascus and other Mohammedan rulers, even taking some towns from them.

During this period, Saladin, Sultan of Egypt, taking advantage of dissension among the crusading princes, attacked them, and took Jerusalem and the rest of Palestine (1187).

Then a new Crusade was started, led by the German Emperor Frederick Barbarossa. This monarch sent emissaries to Leo, asking his help against the Mohammedans, promising him a crown as a reward. Leo supplied the Crusaders with provisions and rendered them other assistance. Barbarossa died without fulfilling his promise, but the crown was sent by his successor, Henry VI., after consultation with the Pope of Rome. Leo was crowned king in 1198. The following year, the new Armenian king also obtained recognition from the Byzantine Emperor, who sent him a crown. Leo still further extended his dominions and put the whole kingdom into excellent condition. He did not, like the Bagratunis, re-establish the régime of the Arsacidae, but tried to imitate European institutions, inviting many French, English, and German experts to his kingdom, giving them appointments in the court, the army, and the council. Many new schools were opened in this reign in which the teaching was entrusted to learned Europeans as well as to Armenians.

Arts and handicrafts, commerce and agriculture also flourished under this king. Leo died in 1219 after a reign of thirty-four years. For his great services to his people, he was called "Leo the Benefactor."

It was under the rule of this king that Armenia entered into close relations with Europe. Just as the Zoroastrian Persians and

170

afterwards the Greeks had inflicted all kinds of persecutions on the Armenians in order to convert them to their religions, so also in the reign of Leo II. and for many years afterwards the popes of Rome did everything possible to make the Armenians join their Church. The popes promised the Armenians help against the Mohammedans, they even offered to organize a Crusade, but the first condition was that the Armenians should become Catholics. When the Armenians did not accept these advances, a number of Catholic priests came to Armenia and tried to convert them. These priests were called "Unitors." At this time the Tartars (who were heathens) became very strong and conquered Persia. The Armenian king when this conquest took place was Hetum. This king, though he maintained friendly relations with the courts of Europe, attached little weight to promises emanating from these quarters; he therefore formed an alliance with the Tartars against the Mohammedans. He tried to indoctrinate his new allies in Christian ideas and almost effected their conversion to Christianity. That he did not quite gain his object is due to external causes. Hetum, in conjunction with the Tartars, fought successfully against many Mohammedan sultans, but the Egyptian mamelukes grew strong and the Tartars became Mohammedans (1302), whereupon enmity arose between them and the Armenians. Three Mohammedan races—Seljuks, Tartars, and mamelukes—one after another attacked Cilicia, devastating the country and plundering many towns. The Armenians asked assistance from the Pope and from European kings; help was promised from France, but it never came, so the Tartars conquered Cilicia and slew its king, who, however, was avenged by his youngest brother, Ashin, who collected an army and drove the Tartars out of the country (1308).

The Mohammedan kingdoms became very powerful at this time. The mamelukes dominated, besides Egypt, Arabia, Palestine, and Syria as far as the Euphrates.

The common aim of all the Mohammedan governments was to destroy the independent kingdom of Armenia, because it was the only Christian state in Asia that was capable of rendering assistance to European sovereigns should any of them enter on a new Crusade in order to gain possession of the Holy Sepulchre.

171

When the mamelukes heard that the European states were planning a new Crusade, they formed an alliance with the Tartars and the Sultan of Iconia and devastated Cilicia. But the Armenians made a brave defense and the mamelukes granted a peace for fifteen years. By this peace it was agreed that the King of Armenia should pay a certain amount of tribute and the mamelukes should restore the places they had taken. Again there was talk of a Crusade, and the Sultan of Egypt again attacked Cilicia. Leo V. (King of Armenia) asked for help from Europe, but the only assistance given was 10,000 florins sent by the King of France and a few sacks of corn from the Pope. This was not what the Armenians wanted; in fact they were again left to their fate. The Mohammedan sultan offered to restore Leo's kingdom if he would swear on the Cross and the Gospels that he would have no dealings with the Crusaders. Leo V. died in 1341, and as he had no children the throne passed to the Lusignan dynasty.

There were only four kings of this dynasty: the last king was Leo VI. (1365-1375). He was taken prisoner when the sultan invaded and devastated Cilicia. Thus ended the kingdom of Armenia. After a few years, through the mediation of John, King of Castille, Leo was set at liberty. He came to Europe to ask for help in regaining his kingdom. There was a talk of a Crusade specially on behalf of the Armenians, but it never went beyond the stage of promises, and the last King of Armenia died in Paris in 1393 and is buried there in the Abbey of St. Celestin.

We have spoken mostly of Cilicia during this period. If we wish to complete the picture of the devastation of Armenia, we must name Zenghis Khan, Tamerlane (1387), and other enemies of the human race, but we will not enter into particulars of their work of desolation.

Silver Age of Armenian Literature

The period whose history we have sketched (twelfth to fourteenth centuries), especially the two former centuries, is called the Silver Age of Armenian literature. The independence of

Armenia gave a breathing space which facilitated the production of literary works. This is the period of the revival of learning and also the period when Armenia came in contact with the countries of Western Europe and became acquainted with Western civilisation.

CATHOLICOS NERSES, surnamed "the Gracious," is the most brilliant author of the beginning of this period (1100-1173). He was the great-grandchild of Grigor Magistros, and his brother Grigorios was Catholicos before him. His songs and sharakans are greatly loved by the people and some of the latter are sung in the churches. He was canonized as a saint. Nerses was the first Armenian to write very long poems. He followed his great-grandfather in using rhyme. There is a great variety of meter in his works. As a rule his long poems are written in eight-feet lines, the same rhyme being employed nearly throughout the poem. This practice he abandoned in certain cases for, as he himself remarks, "it might tire the reader"! He has also poems written in couplets of short lines, which are the most musical and successful of his works. Some of his poems have peculiarities of their own. He sometimes begins the lines of the first stanza with A, those of the next with B, and so on in alphabetical order, or he uses the same letter for the beginning of the first line and the conclusion of the last. He also sometimes makes metrical acrostics of his own name. Of course these contrivances were in common use in his time. Sometimes he makes acrostics of the titles or names in dedications of his poems. But these artificialities do not spoil the poem or give the impression of a tour de force, in fact they are so unobtrusive that they might easily escape the reader's notice. In all he has written 15,000 lines.

One of his long poems entitled Jesus the Son consists of 4000 eight-feet lines. These lines, with very few exceptions, end with the Armenian syllable -in. Some of the songs in this poem are very beautiful and are sung in churches.

Another of his long poems is an elegy on the Fall of Edessa which was taken from the Crusaders by the Turks in 1144. This is an allegory: the town itself recounts its misfortunes and addresses itself to other cities of the world, to the mountains, to the seas, and begs them not to judge her by what she is in her present condition, but assures them that she was once a crown bearer and in a most happy state, but now she is in mourning, and misfortune has befallen her. As Nerses was a contemporary of the event which forms the subject of the poem, the latter has an historical value, being a first-hand source of information relating to the times of the Crusaders.

Nerses also wrote a long poem narrating the history of Armenia from the days of Haik up to his own time. Leo III., one hundred and fifty years after the poet's death, asked the bishop Vahram Rabun to continue the poem from the death of Nerses to his own time (1275), thus giving the annals of the Rubinian dynasty. In writing this sequel, in 1500 lines, he said: "It is a bold act to continue the work of Nerses the Gracious," but he adds that, knowing that with gold thread embroidery black threads are sometimes introduced, he consented to undertake the labour.

It is not within our province here to describe the great work achieved by Nerses in other directions, but he was much beloved by his people and has left an immortal name as the greatest personality of his age. We only here record one incident to show the breadth of his ideas. In the town of Edessa pestilence was raging and sufferers from the disease were taken out of the town and segregated. It was considered hopeless to cure them, as it was believed that the disease came as a punishment from God. Nerses sent out an epistle to the plague-stricken people, offering them consolation, saying that, in compensation for their suffering, they would receive eternal bliss. In this letter, he declares that the disease was not sent from Heaven as a punishment and people should not avoid the sick; on the contrary, it was their duty to care for their brethren when they were in distress, and he assured them that, with patience and right treatment, it was possible to get rid of the disease.

This counsel made an immense impression on the people, as they had the word of the Catholicos that this was not a heaven-sent chastisement; they nursed the patients and in a short time the pestilence was stayed.

174

This idea of Nerses, though it is now commonly held, was very remarkable in the age in which he lived. Nerses the Gracious is considered the Fénelon of Armenia. Some of his elegies are perfect gems of poetic art. One of his prayers is divided into twenty-four verses, according to the twenty-four hours, one verse to be used each hour, but, seeing that this is sometimes impracticable, he says that it might be read in three portions of light verses in the morning, at noon, and at night. If this division is also impossible, he recommends that it should be read in two portions, in the morning and evening. This prayer has been translated into thirty-six languages, of which English is one.

An example of the work of Nerses the Gracious, entitled "The Arrival of the Crusaders," is given in this volume on page 60.

This is hardly a representative poem and is not the best specimen of the author's work. It was inserted because of the interest of the Crusades for Europeans. The gems of his work may be found among the sharakans, which we can say without hesitation will bear comparison with any work of this class in any language of the world. Unfortunately, it is impossible to do justice to these hymns in a translation. Nerses also wrote verses for children, and riddles, both in the vernacular.

In general, his language is simple and expressive. He also composed short fables, according to a contemporary historian; some of these were recited at weddings and other festivals.

Mkhitar Gosh was the author of one hundred and fifty fables, marked by good taste, purity, and elegance. He died in 1213. He is called the Aesop of Armenia.

The following is a specimen of Mkhitar Gosh's fables: The owl sent matchmakers to the eagle, asking his daughter in marriage, in these terms: "You are the ruler of the day; I am the ruler of the night. It will be better for us to form an alliance by marriage."

The proposal was accepted.

175

After the wedding, the bridegroom could not see by day and the bride could not see by night. Therefore the falcons ridiculed them, and their marriage was unhappy.

This fable is meant as a warning against marriages between Christians and pagans.

Many of Mkhitar Gosh's fables are very original and have a charm of their own.

Another famous fabulist was Vardan Aigektzi. His collection of fables is called The Book of the Fox. Several additions have been made to this work by later hands, so that the book has no uniformity of style and some fables in the collection are childish and trivial.

This is one of the fables in this book:

Mankind is like three fools. The first went to the tops of the mountains trying to catch a wind, and take it home, but though he tried a hundred years he never caught a wind that was as big as a drop of rain. The second, taking with him a number of servants and a great deal of money, sat down by the side of a river, trying to use its waters as a tablet on which to inscribe an elegy, but he could not form a word or trace a letter, though he labored for a hundred years. The third tried to surpass the others by undertaking two enterprises at once. He had a huge bow made with arrows to match, and tried by night to shoot at the stars and other heavenly bodies and bring them home, that he alone might have light, but he could not catch a spark. Besides this, during the day he ran after his own shadow, but never caught it, though he tried for a hundred years.

The moral of this fable is the futility of human life and human endeavor. "Vanity of vanities; all is vanity."

MOSES KAGHANKATVATZI (seventh century) mentions in his history some interesting fables. In one of them, which arose when there was a great famine in the land, the story is put into the mouth of a personification of the grain millet, whose narrative is to this effect:—

"I, Millet, was lying in an unknown place in the village of Kaku, in the province of Shakashen. All the purchasers treated me with contempt and rejected me. Then came my brother, Famine, and dominated the land. From that day I went and sat on the tables of the King and the Catholicos."

Armenian apologues and proverbial sayings are worthy of attention. Here are a few characteristic specimens; some of these are rhymed in the original, in others the contrasted words rhyme:—

One fool threw a stone into a well; forty wise men were unable to get it out.

He crossed the sea safely, and was drowned in a brook.

They were reading the Gospel over the wolf's head. He said: "Hurry up! The sheep will get past."

They asked the partridge: "Why are your feet red?" "From the cold," he replied. "We have seen you in the summer as well," they rejoined.

Are you the corn of the upper field? (Who are you that you should be set above others?)

A black cat has passed between them. (Referring to friends who have quarreled.)

Whenever you touch a stone, may it become gold! (A blessing.)

The donkey began its tricks on the bridge.

Light for others, fire for the house. (A saint abroad, a devil at home.)

The black donkey is tied up at the gate. (A worthless thing is always at hand.)

Here is a riddle by Nerses Shnorhali:—

I saw an outspread white tent, wherein black hens were perched, that laid eggs of various kinds and spoke in human language. (A book.)

Between the end of the thirteenth century and the beginning of the fourteenth lived, almost contemporaneously, three great poets, all ecclesiastics: — CONSTANTINE ERZINGATZI, HOVHANNES ERZINGATZI, and FRIK, who were almost the last singers of the dying Armenian kingdom.

The first of these, CONSTANTINE ERZINGATZI, was born about 1250-1260 in Erzingan. From early youth he showed poetic talent and gained favor from the people, but incurred the jealousy of his own associates. In one of his poems he says he cannot tell why his enemies hate him and expresses a desire to know their reason. Erzingatzi had a friend, a certain Amir Tol, who lived in Tabriz. Erzingatzi used to send his poems, as he wrote them, to this friend, who entered them in a book. The poems in this collection number twenty-two. The manuscript is preserved in the library of St. Lazare, Venice. The themes of Erzingatzi's poems are—among other things—the love of the rose and the nightingale, the beauty of nature, the wedding of the flowers, spring, dawn, and morning. In his love poems, he throws over his emotions a mystic veil of celestial hue, and some of his lines rise to a higher level than ordinary amorous verse. For him, love and beauty are one and the same. He says that one who is without love has no sense of beauty. He calls his lady-love a breeze of spring, and himself a thirsty flower, but a flower on which only a hot southern blast is ever blowing, so that his love-thirst continually endures. He likens his mistress to the radiant heavenly bodies—the sun, moon, and stars—but her light is stronger than that of all other luminaries, for it alone can illumine his darkened heart.

Erzingatzi says that, if he is to have any share in the life of love in

178

this world, he will be content with one hour of "morning love" that springs from the heart. For that he is willing to exchange his life. He prays to God for such love, always emphasizing the word "morning."

Among his works is a beautiful poem on Spring, which begins with a hundred thousand thanksgivings for the blessing that has flown down from heaven to earth:—

"It was dark and every stone was ice-bound; there was not a green herb, but now the earth arrays itself anew. The winter was like a prison, the spring like a sun that rises in the night. Everything is merry and joyous; even the dew-bringing cloud thunders gently, spanning the earth with its bow and causing many swift rivers to flow, which, without distinction, throw into rapturous intoxication all places of the earth.

"Terribly roar the streams that come down from the mountains, but, after strolling to and fro among the meadows in loving fashion, pass on to touch the face of the sea.

"The birds sing sweetly; the swallow chants psalms, the lark comes, reciting the praise of the morning. All leap into life— plants, birds, beasts with their offspring; they all form themselves into one great flock and dance together. The flowers have assembled in the garden. The Nightingale, proclaiming the glad things of the great resurrection, also enters the garden, seeking the Rose.

"When the time is ripe, she opens, and the other flowers, when they see the splendor of the Rose, run off, over hill and dale, and, from fear, lose their color. The Nightingale is intoxicated with the sweet odor of the Rose. Then takes place a festival of nature and the Rose sings her own praise."

The original text of this poem is a real achievement as regards language, poetical expressions, and art, showing that Erzingatzi was a master of his craft.

Erzingatzi was also the author of a long narrative poem, called

179

Farman and Asman, recounting the love adventures of a Persian princess. This was composed at the request of a Syrian knight and shows some traces of Persian influence.

Another long narrative poem of this writer, entitled A Girl's Questions, seems to owe something to Arabic literature.

Erzingatzi is also the author of many didactic poems. Here are a few stanzas from another of his poems:—

> "Waken from your dreams
> And behold, you that were sleeping,
>   How through all the night
> They their sleepless watch are keeping.
>   Ever circling round
> By the will of God who made them:
>   And heaven's arches wide
> To uplift and hold He bade them.
>
> "I awoke from sleep
> And a while I stood and waited.
>   When the long night passed,
> When appeared the dawn belated,—
>   Many stars of light
> Watching stood to greet the morning;
>   Servants of our God,
> All the sky of night adorning.
>
> "Then a Star arose
> Near the Morning Star, in Heaven;
>   Fairer than all stars,
> Radiance to that Star was given.
>
> "When the moon beheld
> She bade all the stars to vanish.
>
> All turned pale, and set,
> As she spoke their light to banish.
>   Cleared was heaven's face
> And the sun arose in splendor;

Then a Child appeared,
Sweet the Name He had, and tender." [33]

HOVHANNES ERZINGATZI (b. 1250) was educated in a monastery on the confines of Georgia and Armenia under a bishop who was renowned for his learning. He returned to Erzingan in 1272 and traveled to Jerusalem in 1281, in the course of his journey passing through Cilicia in order to visit the Armenian royal seat, where King Leon was then reigning. By his learning and talents he attracted the attention of the Catholicos, who appointed him director of all the schools in the city.

By order of the Catholicos, he wrote a grammar, remarkable for its clear and comprehensible style and language. He also came under the notice of the king. At the annual horse race two of the king's sons were among the competitors. On this occasion Erzingatzi made a speech, which left a great impression and gained him recognition as an orator. In Cilicia he learnt Latin and made several translations from that language into Armenian. He wrote many Biblical commentaries, besides other religious and devotional works, as well as treatises on astrology; but his fame rests chiefly on his verse. In addition to religious and moral poems, he wrote love songs, and lays relating to nature. In his ethical as well as in his love poems we find quaint metaphors and similes.

As, for instance, in the following stanza, where our poet seems to be forestalling Bunyan:—

"All my sins I once amassed
And sat down before them weeping.
     When the caravan went past
With my load I followed, leaping.
     Then an angel that we met,
'Woful pilgrim, whither farest?
     Thou wilt there no lodging get
With that burden that thou bearest.'"

---

[33] All the metrical translations quoted are by Miss Z. C. Boyajian. Like her other translations in this volume they are almost literal renderings, and the original metre has been kept.

In another poem, entitled "Like an Ocean is this World," which appears on page 61 of this volume, he uses the metaphor afterwards employed in Donne's Hymn to Christ and Tennyson's Crossing the Bar.

His love poems are exquisitely fresh and rich.

The aesthetic character of his love and his enthusiasm for beauty are shown by his declaration, in one of the poems, after a rapturous expression of his passion for a lady of whom he gives a rich-hued word-portrait, that the only thing that keeps his feelings within bounds is the knowledge that, after death, her face will wither and its colors fade.

In 1284 he went to Tiflis, the capital town of Georgia, where he gave, in the newly-built church, on the occasion of its opening, a discourse on the movements of the heavenly bodies. This subject had a great fascination for him and he treated it in a manner that deeply impressed his hearers, including the king's son who was present. His discourse was not a sermon, but a poetical oration. On the prince's asking him to write a poem on the same subject, he wrote one of a thousand lines. At the desire of another prince, he composed another poem on the same theme.

KHACHATUR KECHARETZI (better known by his pen-name, FRIK) was a priest who was born at the end of the thirteenth century and died about 1330. He wrote many poems, several of which are of an allegorical character; also laments on the state of his country, and several mystic and other religious poems, as well as love songs; but his most characteristic work is the poem addressed to God, asking why He is unmindful of the terrible condition of the Armenian nation, and also enumerating the inequalities of the world, showing how the wicked prosper and the righteous suffer.

"If we are useless creatures?" (he says) "unworthy of Thy care, why dost Thou not entirely destroy us?"

An extract from this long poem is given in this volume on page 5.

End of Armenian Kingdom

At the close of the fourteenth century, the glory of Cilicia vanished, as the Armenian kingdom became extinct, after an existence of nearly three hundred years; and Armenia once more became the scene of turmoil and bloodshed.

The fifteenth century opened with the invasion of Tamerlane, when the country was again desolated and subdued. This was a century of the overthrow of Eastern civilization.

The Byzantine Empire, shaken from its foundation, was dashed to pieces, and its capital, Constantinople, fell into the hands of the Ottomans (1453), a new Mohammedan power, which aspired to become master of the whole of Asia. The Turcomans and, later, the Persians, tried to check the advance of the Turks into their territories. Hence commenced a long series of wars between the two Mohammedan states which continued through four centuries, and Armenia passed now into the hands of the one, now into the hands of the other. The country was again the scene of war, wherein reigned desolation, fire, and death.

After the occupation of Constantinople, Turkish influence extended over most of the eastern part of Armenia.

Renaissance

From this time, migrations of Armenians out of their own country into different parts of the world became more frequent.

Twenty years after the invention of printing (1476) a grammar in many tongues was published in France, which contains several pages in Armenian.

In 1512 the first Armenian printed book was issued in Venice. After that Armenians set up presses in various countries.

Notwithstanding the political position of the country, its poetry continued to flourish and assumed a definite character; and the voices of the poets rose continually louder and louder. This century, together with the two preceding and the two following ones, forms a flourishing age for poetry.

The chief poets of this century are:—Hovhannes Tulkourantzi, Mkrtich Naghash, Grigoris of Aghtamar, Nahapet Kouchak, Arakel Sunetzi.

HOVHANNES TULKOURANTZI (1450-1525) was Catholicos of Sis. He is a poet of the days of spring, flowers, beauty, love. He wrote also moral and religious poems, besides other things. He cannot understand how it is possible for one who loves a beautiful woman to grow old and die.

"Whosoever loves you, how can he die? How can his face grow pale in death?"

He sings of the sanctity of family life, warning his readers against the strange woman "who brings torment and grief. Even his lawful wife brought trouble to Adam; what then is to be expected of the stranger?"

He has a striking poem on Death, which he addresses thus:—

"There is nothing so bitter as thou, no venom is more bitter; only Hell surpasseth thee, and it is thou who bringest Hell in thy train. Solomon remembered thee, saying, 'Of what profit is my wisdom? Say not I am a King possessing gold and treasures.'

"Alas, O death! thou hast a grudge against the sons of Adam and thou avengest thyself on them.

"Thou didst not consider that Moses was a prophet, nor art thou ashamed of assaulting David; thou takest even Father Abraham; thou draggest King Tiridates from his throne; and thou respectest not the Emperor Constantine.

"If a hero is attended by 1000 horsemen and arrayed in six coats

184

of armor, thou shootest thine arrows at him and bringest him down, then thou castest him into prison and before the entrance thou placest a great stone."

The poem continues:—

> "Like an eagle flying far,
> Forth on wide-spread wings thou farest;
> All the strong ones of the earth
> In thy wing-tips rolled thou bearest."

In other poems we see his susceptibility to passion and his sense of love's power. In one of these poems he depicts [34] a bishop of 100 years old whose beard had turned from white to yellow and who, when officiating at the altar, suddenly uttered the name of a lady in his invocation before the cross.

MKRTICH NAGHASH was Archbishop of Diarbekr. He lived when the country was in difficult political circumstances. His talents were appreciated not only by Armenians, but also by the Mohammedan rulers with whom, thanks to his tact, he established friendly relations, whereby he was able to protect his compatriots from many oppressions. He built a church, which he adorned with beautiful pictures of his own painting. But, after the death of the Mohammedan princes who were his patrons, tyranny and oppression began again under their successors. He went to Byzantium to solicit aid for his suffering countrymen, but returned disappointed.

Besides his artistic skill, he was a poet of considerable merit. His poems are generally on moral and religious themes—the vanity of the world, avarice, and so forth; he also wrote songs of exile, and love songs.

In his poem on avarice he says that that vice is the root of all evil: "Kings and princes are continually fighting against one another, watering the country with blood. They destroy flourishing towns;

---

[34] In the Armenian Church there are two classes of clergy--the higher order to which bishops belong and who do not marry, and the lower order of parish priests who do marry.

they drive the inhabitants into exile; and spread desolation wherever they go; and all this is through avarice."

He goes on to specify other evils springing from this sin.

In the love songs of Mkrtich Naghash, the Rose and the Nightingale whisper to each other fiery love speeches complaining of each other's cruelty. Then they admonish each other not to let their passion consume them, and sing each other's praises.

This is an extract from one of his songs of exile: "The thoughts of an exile from his country are wanderers like himself. If his mind is wiser than Solomon's, if his words are precious pearls, in a foreign land they bid him be silent and call him an ignorant fool. His death is as bitter as his life; there is no one to cross his hands over his heart; they laugh as they cover him with earth; no mourner follows him to the grave. But I, Naghash, say that an exile's heart is tender. In a foreign land, what is sweet seems gall; the rose becomes a thorn. Speak gently to an exile; give him a helping hand, and you will expiate your sins which rankle like thorns."

These songs of exile (or pilgrim songs) are a special feature of Armenian poetry and for ages have been written by various poets. They are original and often quaint and express the feelings of Armenians who live far from their native mountains and fields, showing how they pine for the land of their birth, reflecting the natural beauties of their fatherland, and their yearning for their hearth and the dear faces of home.

In 1469 in the town of Mardin there was an epidemic of smallpox, which caused many deaths. He thus describes one of the victims: "A youth beautiful to see, the image of the sun; his brows were arches; his eyes like lamps guiding him by their light. This lovely child lay on the ground, writhing piteously, looking to right and left, while the terrible Angel of Death was busily engaged in loosing the cords of his soul. Then the boy cried, saying: 'Pity me and save me from the hands of this holy angel, for I am young.' Then he turned to his father, and asking help

186

from him, said: 'There are a thousand desires in my heart and not one of them fulfilled.'

"The father answered: 'I would not begrudge gold and silver for thy redemption; but these are of no avail. I would willingly give my life for thine.' In the end the light of the child's life was extinguished; the lovely hue of his face faded; his sea-like eyes lost their luster; the power of his graceful arm was cut off."

Here is a translation in verse of a poem on a mysterious Flower:—

"All the lovely flowers that were
One by one have left and gone,
One Flower too there was that went
Mourned and wept by every one.
    Sweetest fragrance had that Flower,
    Scent that filled the earth and air,
    So that all the flowers of earth
    Sought in love this Blossom fair.
Some for this sweet Flow'ret's sake
Paled and withered languidly;

Many for this Flow'ret's sake
Blossomed like the almond tree.
    God Himself had sent that Flower,
    But all did not know its worth.
    He that gave took back His own,
    Many wept upon the earth.
And the Flower went to a place
Where all flowers rejoiced and smiled;
Flowers of many a brilliant hue
With its sweetness it beguiled.
    From its beauty other flowers
    Borrowed luster, and they glowed;
    Every blossom in its kind
    To that Flower knelt and bowed."

GRIGORIS OF AGHTAMAR was born about 1418 and was Catholicos of Aghtamar, an island in the Lake of Van, which has picturesque surroundings fit to inspire a poet; so that it is not surprising that our Catholicos became a singer animated by poetic fire, the exponent of love and beauty—of the Nightingale and the Rose.

It is evident, from his works, that Grigoris had a great love of life. We see this especially in a poem entitled The Gardener and his Garden. The Gardener, says the poet, enters his garden every morning and hears the sweet voice of the nightingale as he examines the newly planted flowers of various colors. This beautiful spot he surrounds with a hedge, bringing stones from the river, thorns from the mountain. He has just built arbors, made a fountain, introduced little running brooks, and planted vines, when, all of a sudden, a voice utters the command: "Come out of thy garden." It is Death who beckons him out. He expostulates: "I have not yet seen life and light; I have not yet seen the fruit of the garden; I have not yet smelt the rose; I have not yet drunk my wine or filled my casks; I have not plucked flowers for a nosegay. I have not yet rejoiced over my garden."

But his prayers are not heeded; obedient to the unchangeable law of the universe, he at last capitulates to the Angel of Death.

After describing the Gardener's death and burial, the poet goes on to tell what happens to the garden after its owner has left it; the rose fades; the other flowers disappear; the hedge is broken down, and what was once a lovely garden becomes a scene of desolation.

This is his description of the face of his lady-love. He likens her eyebrows to a sword; the sparkle of her eyes to a sharp lance; her eyes to the sunlit sea. She is, he says, as straight as a willow; her lips are like harp strings; her teeth, a row of pearls; her tongue is sugar; and, wherever she rests, the place becomes a garden. She has fragrance sweeter than the violet of the spring; she is like a white rose, pure and sweet, like a newly opened flower; a young almond plant. Her face is red and white, like an apple of the forest. She soars high, like a daring eagle. She is brilliant as a peacock with golden feathers.

We have in this volume (page 55) a translation of one of Grigoris' longer poems, entitled "Concerning the Rose and the Nightingale," in which it is interesting to note that—quaintly enough—the poet gives the text of a letter sent with great pomp, by special messengers, to the Rose; adding the consequence which followed, and the verbal answer returned.

The subject of the Rose and the Nightingale is a Persian one originally, but the outstanding characteristics of the Armenian versions consist in the refinements and subtleties of the feelings described, the deference paid to the Rose, and the idea of continuity and faithfulness in love. These feelings are minutely described in this beautiful poem, and summed up in the Rose's message to the Nightingale on p. 58:—

> "I cannot there return immediately;
> A little he must wait, in patient wise:
> But if his love is perfectly with me,
> Tell him to look for it in Paradise."

These ideals constitute the difference between the mentality of Mohammedanism and Christianity.

NAHAPET KOUCHAK was a fine poet of the seventeenth century. He is called the Psalmist of Love. Although there is a slight resemblance in style between his writings and those of the Persian poets, his poetry is original. The works attributed to him have only recently been published as a whole; they have been translated into French and other languages, and greatly admired. Some critics have placed him higher than Sadi and other Persian poets. (Examples of his work are given on pages 9, 10, and 34.)

ARAKEL SUNETZI was the Metropolitan of the province of Suni. He appears to have possessed a thorough acquaintance with the writings of his time. His chief work is the Book of Adam, a long narrative poem, telling the story of the Fall in the style of a romance in which theology, lyrics, heroic lays, and folklore are all fused together.

Adam, though because of his great love for his wife he was

189

inclined to yield to her petition, yet wavered, not knowing whether to hearken to his spouse or to his Creator. "But his mind went with his eyes; he deserted God, but not the woman; for, without Eve, half of his body was dead, and with the other half it was impossible to live."

Among the lyrics in this book is one entitled The Rib, of which we subjoin two stanzas:—

> "The rib is bow-shaped, so her face,
> Sped by her looks, is like a dart;
> Who gazeth on a woman's grace,
> No salve or drug can cure his smart.

> "And for the rib is high and low—
> One side is vaulted, one is round,
> Her face doth love and sweetness show
> Whilst in her heart fierce hate is found."

Here is a passage from another poem of Sunetzi's entitled The Glory of the Saints, describing the Resurrection:—

> "Opened are the tombs;
> Now rise the dead that long in dust have lain.
>   Decked with brilliant hues,
> Bright as the sun, they cannot fade again.
>   While the earth, renewed,
> Doth greet the Lord, all fresh and dazzling white;
>   And the heavens are decked
> More richly than before, sevenfold more bright.
>   Then in heaven shines forth
> With arms stretched out like rays, the Holy Rood.
>   With the Cross appear
> The hosts of fire—a countless multitude.
>   Butterflies dance forth
> Amongst the angels—none may mark them out."

In the sixteenth century, Turkish and Persian wars became fiercer and the Armenian history of this century becomes the record of the sufferings of the country during these wars. Poets of this period were Nerses Mokatzi, Minas Tokhatzi, Ghazar of Sebastia, Sarkavak Bertaktzi.

NERSES MOKATZI was an ecclesiastic and poet. Very few of his works have come down to us. One of the poems we have—entitled The Dispute between Heaven and Earth—is interesting. The poet begins by saying that Heaven and Earth are brothers. One day these brothers disputed as to which of them was the greater. "Of course," says the poet, "the Heaven is high, but the Earth is more fruitful."

He then goes on to report a dialogue between the brothers in which each enumerates his own possessions, declaring them superior to those of the other. The following is a short prose summary of this dialogue:—

> Heaven. Surely I possess more than you. The stars, with their radiance, are all in my domain.
> Earth. The flowers, with their six thousand colors, are in mine.
> Heaven. If I withhold my dew, how will your flowers array themselves?
> Earth. You derive your dew from the sea, which originates in me. If I cut off the source of the sea, how would you get your dew?
> Heaven. I have something else that you have not: should I veil my sun your flowers would fade.
> Earth. Oh, I will bring forth waters from my abyss to keep my flowers alive.
> Heaven. The lightning and the hail could destroy your flowers if I willed it so.
> Earth. I have mountains and valleys that would intercept them and shield the flowers.
> Heaven. All brave and wise men are buried in your depths.
> Earth. When God recalls the souls that are His, what is to be done? If I did not receive and conceal their bodies, the angels would flee from the deathly odor, and Heaven and Earth would be shaken.
> Heaven. The Nine Orders of Angels are all here with me.
> Earth. In my realm are the Apostles and Prophets.

Heaven. I am the Heaven of Seven Regions; the Sun, the Moon, and the Creator-God sitting on His throne all have their abode in me.

Earth. Your Seven Regions will be shaken from their foundation. The Sun, the Moon, and the Stars will be cast into the darkness and your Creator-God, with His throne, will descend to me. The Judgment will be held in my domain.

> "Heaven then bent down its head
> To the Earth in adoration,
> You too, children of the Earth,
> Bow to her in adoration.
> What is higher than the Earth
> Praise and love bring to enwreathe her.
> For to-day we walk on her
> And to-morrow sleep beneath her."

This poem is interesting, as it breathes the spirit of the revival of popular poetry, with its worship of nature, beauty, and love, of which things the Earth is the personification. Hence the poet exalts Earth above Heaven. Here we see also a change of ideas. The older Christian poets were churchmen and sang contempt of the present world and concentration on the joys of heaven. This new note, struck from the beginning of the fifteenth century, gradually grows bolder, and sounds forth daringly, as we hear it in this poem, which seems all the more remarkable when we remember that its author was a priest. This is the song, not of a lover of vanities, but, rather, of an enthusiast, who loves beauty and has learnt that it is good to live on the earth, because it also contains beautiful things that are worth living for. This poem also shows the conquest of learning and science which, at the time it was written, had found their way into Armenia as well as elsewhere, perhaps through the new Armenian colonies formed in Europe and other parts of the world.

MINAS TOKHATZI, a humorous poet, lived in Poland. He wrote verses on Toothache and on Tobacco (descanting on its objectionable odor and showing how the smoker becomes its slave); also on Flies.

To convey an idea of his art, we give the substance of the last-named work:—

"The flies," says the poet, "for some reason or other, went forth to combat against me. They also entered into a conspiracy with my penknife. Knowing of this, I implored the knife not to listen to the accursed insects, who had already caused me enough pain. The attack was begun in a novel fashion; the flies came, buzzing, in gay and merry mood, and settled on my hands and arms in a friendly manner, asking me to write them something in red ink. At the same time, the penknife, playing me a perfidious trick, cut my hand. I protested against this treatment. The penknife justified itself by saying it had acted thus because I had told a lie. I got a few moments' rest, after this, from the flies, till, at dinnertime, I met with three of them, who announced that more were coming. The combat was renewed. During the night, the flies were relieved by their allies, the fleas."

GHAZAR OF SEBASTIA, an ecclesiastic, has fallen under the spell of some eyes " as deep as the sea." He describes the torment under which he is pining away and his longing for his mistress's arrival, like the longing of a patient for his physician. The face of his love (he says) is like glistening amber; her eyes are so bewitching, that

"The sun and moon have unto thee come down,
Lovingly on thy locks they hang, and gleam;
And clustering stars thy beauteous forehead crown,
Aflame and drunken with thy love they seem."/

There is nothing known of SARKAVAK BERTAKTZI, but this poem from his pen is interesting

"O vine, you should commended be
For you are beautiful to see;
Your fruit is of all fruits most fair:—
The crown and diadem they wear.
Like strands of gold your branches spread,
Like ropes of pearl the grapes they thread.
For some are dark and some are white,

And some are red, transmitting light.
Some glow like amber in the dusk,
Perfumed with frankincense and musk.
Left us by the Creator's care,—
From Eden's fields a keepsake rare.
To us on earth you seem to be
The fruit of immortality.
To Noah you were by angels borne
His heart to gladden and adorn.
Your fruit when gathered from the vine
Unto the wine-press we assign;
Your juice like crimson roses glows
And through the press in torrents flows.
Then into jars we pour the meath,
There without fire to boil and seethe.
How many kings around you press,
Your name how many princes bless!
The Sovereign's heart you fill with joy,
With power to conquer and destroy;
If he is wroth with any man,
And places him beneath his ban,
One drop of you immediately
Would move his heart to set him free.
The man that from his birth was blind,
Drinking of you, his sight doth find;
Of glorious cities he can tell,
Wherein his footsteps never fell.
The dumb, that halted in his speech,
To prate with fluency you teach.
More glibly than a parrot, he
Will jest and wanton dotingly.
At mass, within the sacred cup,
The holy priest doth raise you up.
Disease and pain through you will cease,
By you all sinners find release.
To town and village you are borne,
To convent, wilderness forlorn;
Where men do not your sparkle see,
No mass nor service can there be."

The seventeenth century resembles its predecessor as regards the political position of Armenia, except that the misery is even greater.

Eighteenth Century and Onward

During the last years of the eighteenth century, the Russian conquest of Armenia began.

At the end of the eighteenth century an Armenian monk named MKHITAR SEPASTATZI established at St. Lazare in Venice an Armenian Brotherhood, who devoted themselves to literature. This Brotherhood is still in existence, and has a branch in Vienna. During this period of more than a century its members have printed hundreds of old MSS. of historical value. They have also produced many works dealing with history and other branches of learning, and translations of foreign classics, thus rendering a great service to Armenian literature.

It will be remembered that Byron stayed at St. Lazare and studied Armenian. He actually took part in the publication of an Armenian-English dictionary and grammar.

For centuries music and song have become a joy to Armenians through minstrels called ashoughs. Ashoughs are invited to all weddings and other festivities, where they are the life of the party and the makers of merriment. They sing also on the bridges and in the squares, and wander from courtyard to courtyard. Their song is not always merry; it is sometimes sad, sometimes even bitter. They always carry with them their saz or tar or kamancha, oriental instruments, on which they accompany their songs. Many of the ashoughs are blind. To be an ashough is considered a high attainment. In order to acquire the art, any one who aspires to become an ashough first observes a fast of seven weeks, then goes to the monastery of Sourb Karapet, which is the Parnassus of Armenian musicians. "Sourb Karapet" is John the Baptist, who is the patron saint of Armenian minstrels. In the

Near East, ashoughs (who are mostly Armenians) are greatly admired not only by Armenians, but by Persians, Turks, and other races, as some of them sing in other languages besides Armenian. Some ashoughs sing their own verses, but as a rule the songs are the composition of a special class of poets. The songs of these other ashoughs often reveal deep feelings and many of them are high-class poems.

As a typical ashough author, I will only mention SAYAT NOVA. His lyre attained extreme sweetness; he combines all the vivid coloring of the East with soft and refined shading. He was born in 1712. He was a special favorite at the court of the Georgian king. In his own words, he "sat in the palace among the beauties and sang to them," but his songs seem not merely to be poems in praise of court beauties, or for their amusement; they seem an expression of the deep feelings of his heart. A word-picture of his lady-love will be found on page 75 of this volume ("Thy Voice is Sweet").

His love is so intense that one sees at once that he is capable of deep feelings and one is drawn to him; yet this love is pure and unselfish. He describes his love as a sea and himself as a little barque floating on it. For ten years he has wooed the lady as a prince, but without success; he will not relinquish the pursuit of her, but resolves now for seven years to pay court to her in the character of a pilgrim-minstrel.

He is even content only to sleep on her doorstep. There is something else that is a part of his life, namely, his kamancha. He threatens to cut the strings of his instrument if he is a week without seeing his beloved.

Once he comes face to face with his lady-love and says:—

"What avails me now a physician? The ointment burns, and does not heal the wound, but your medicine is a different one."

But she replies that she has no remedy for him. In another poem he is in despair, and says:—

"Without thee, of what use is the world's wealth? I will don the habit of a monk and visit the monasteries one by one. Perhaps in one of them I shall discover a way of redemption from my hopeless love." (See "Without Thee what are Song and Dance to Me?" on page 87 of this volume.)

In another poem he expresses the wavering between earthly and heavenly life, saying:—

"If one obeys the will of the soul, then the body is offended. How shall I escape this sorrow?

At last he carries out his declaration and becomes a monk. He secludes himself from the world in a lonely monastery, far away from Tiflis; but once he hears that a minstrel has come to that city whom none can equal, whereupon he steals out of the monastery, disguised as a layman, and taking his saz with him, goes to Tiflis, enters into contest with the new minstrel, and conquering him, saves the honor of his native town.

In 1795 Agha Mohammed Khan laid waste Tiflis and many other towns of that region. His soldiers entered the monastery where Sayat Nova was praying and commanded him to come out and become a Mohammedan if he wished to save his life; but he replied, in verse, that he was an Armenian and would not deny his Christ. He was therefore martyred on the spot. Other poems of his appear on pages 38 ("I have a Word I fain would say"), 18 ("I beheld my Love this Morning"), 103 ("Thou art so Sweet").

Characteristics of Armenian Poetry

We have given specimens of mediaeval Armenian poetry; we now proceed to indicate in outline its most striking characteristics.

The theme of the Armenian pagan minstrels was the heroic deeds of their country's history. The adoption of Christianity imparted to Armenian poetry a specific form and tone. At the same time it was the revival of the old Armenian valor, which, strengthened by the circumstances in which the Armenians lived, produced a religious poetry of great purity of feeling, and of a depth and solemnity unequalled by any other poetry of this class.

In the Middle Ages, the poetry gave expression to the love and other emotions of the Armenian poets.

A new poetry of the now Mohammedan Persia written in modern Persian came into being almost simultaneously with the Armenian poetry of the Middle Ages.

Firdusi, Omar Khayyam, Sadi, Hafiz, with a splendid retinue of less famed singers, made Persian the language of verse which, together with Arabic poetry in its earlier stages, no doubt had some influence on the Armenian poets of the Middle Ages; but this influence affected form rather than spirit or character.

Armenian mediaeval poetry does not possess the burning hues of oriental verse, and is perhaps less luxurious, but the grace, charm, ease, and fancy of the Armenian lays are inimitable, and their originality and occasional quaintness are so marked that one feels there is a magic in them. These characteristics are the outcome of the mutual assimilation of eastern and western art, so that the poetry of Armenia, like its language, its art, its Church, stands by itself.

In comparing Armenian with Persian and Arabic poetry, one must remember that the Armenians, as Christians, were not polygamists; and that, to them, marriage was sanctified by the law of God and man. This is what the great Persian poet Sadi says of women: "Choose a fresh wife every spring, or every New Year's day, for the almanac of last year is good for nothing." It would have been impossible for any Armenian poet to entertain such an idea as that.

Whereas women are so cheap in the eyes of the Persian poet, Armenian girls endowed with beauty were considered by their parents and the community very precious possessions, to be zealously guarded, as they were in constant danger of attracting the attention of their Mohammedan lords and being forcibly carried off into harems. This fact had the effect of mingling compassion with the Armenian poets' admiration of a girl's beauty and made them write more feelingly of women.

It must also be remembered that, whereas Mohammedanism looks upon woman as a soulless being, in the eyes of a Christian she possesses a soul as precious as that of a man.

It is an interesting fact that love poems were written by the clergy, often by ecclesiastics of high position, who, by the law of the Armenian Church, are vowed to celibacy. One explanation of this is that they were born poets, and only regarded love as one among many feelings fitted to be the subject of verse. Their use of the first person is only dramatic.

There are also many folksongs which differ, in style and character, from the love-songs of poets. The spirit of these songs is that of Armenian pagan poems. The following is an example of songs of this class. It describes the adventure of a girl.

> "I beheld a youth to-day
> As at dawn I walked unheeding,
>   And the youth stopped on his way,
> Struck my cheek, and left it bleeding.
>   Then my mother questioned me,
> 'Who was it that struck you?' saying,
>   "Twas a thorn, as near the tree
> With the roses I was playing.'
>   'May the tree turn dry and sear
> Which thy pretty cheek left bleeding!
>   'Mother, dear, oh, do not speak,
> 'Twas a youth that stopped to kiss it.
>   'Twas for luck he kissed my cheek,
> If thou curse him he will miss it!'"

Armenian religious and devotional poetry has characteristics of its own. This class of literature falls into two divisions. In the first division are works of a purely literary character written in old Armenian; in the second, works meant for popular use, written in the language of the people. These latter are written in a more familiar style, proverbs and paraphrases being often introduced, in a picturesque fashion, which appeals to the unlearned.

As an example of the popular class of literature we give an extract from a poem about Gregory the Illuminator, who was cast by King Tiridates into a well infested with serpents and other loathsome creatures:—

> "'Take the saint and put him into the prison where dragon-serpents are assembled.'
> They took the saint and put him in the prison where the dragon-serpents were assembled.
> And the poisonous serpents inclined their tongues in worship.
> And said: 'Pity us, O Saint Gregory, and hearken to the complaint of us, dragon-serpents.
> It is many thousands of years since we drank water from the springs;
> We have not drunk water from the springs, but only the blood of condemned men.
> We have eaten no green herbs, but only the flesh of the condemned.'"

The poet goes on to tell how St. Gregory when he came out of the well set free the dragon-serpents in answer to their prayer.

This poem is very old, being written in the fifth or sixth century at the latest. The metre is that of the pagan poets.

We cite here another poem of this class—an allegorical description of Christ on the Cross

> "A little Bird I saw—a peerless One
> Upon the four-armed Sign, that peer hath none.
> O Peerless One, who is like Thee, Thou Peerless One?
>   Thou alone.

> "Its silvery wings were of a matchless white
> More brilliant than the sun's clear, matchless light.

O Matchless One, who is like Thee, Thou Matchless One?
      Thou alone.

"Piteous Its voice—a great, transcendent sigh;
Mighty, as Gabriel's transcendent cry.
Transcendent One, who is like Thee, Transcendent One?
      Thou alone.

"Within Its eyes, gem-like, unrivalled tears;
Surpassing those the morn unrivalled wears;
Unrivalled One, who is like Thee, Unrivalled One?
      Thou alone."

A characteristic species of Armenian poetry is the lullaby. There are hundreds of old Armenian cradle-songs which are still sung by mothers to their infants, and they are exquisitely dainty and sweet.

Here are some stanzas from one of these songs:—

    "Thou art lovely, feet and all,
Whom wouldst have to be thy playmate?
    Hush, the silver moon I'll call—
The bright star to be thy playmate.

"Crimson rose and petals wide,
Thou hast bloomed, our garden's pride.
As many suns shine on thy years
As the leaves our garden bears.

"Oror, hush, the deer are here,
The deer have come from the hills so high,
Have brought sweet sleep to my baby dear,
And filled it in his deep, deep eye."

There are series of Armenian folksongs for every event in life— birth, marriage, death, and so on.

The following is a folksong of death, being the lament of a mother over her dead son:—

"As to-night I walked alone
To the earth my ear inclining,
From the ground I heard a moan,—
My son's voice I heard repining.
'Do not leave me in the ground,
With the serpents round me crawling.

"Food in plenty we have found,"
To their young ones they are calling,
"From his ribs we'll gnaw the flesh,
From his eyes drink water fresh.'"
All the night I found no rest,
I cried out, 'Give me a knife,
I will plunge it in my breast,
I will have no more of life!'"

Yet another feature of the literature of this period is the contemporary history in verse. We come across metrical narratives of great events written by those who experienced them. There is a long and vivid description in verse, by an eye-witness, of the siege of Constantinople. The poet is Abraham Vardapet.

There are also agricultural and craft songs, which are sung by workmen over their labor.

These songs are adapted to the movements necessitated by each occupation.

Another marked difference between Armenian and Mohammedan literature is that Armenians are entirely free from the fatalism which is a distinctive feature of the Mohammedan view of life.

Sadi relates, in his Gulistan, the story of a fisherman that gives the Mohammedan conception of Fate. This fisherman had caught a fish which his strength did not allow him to drag to shore. Fearing to be drawn into the river himself, he abandoned his line, and the fish swam away with the bait in his mouth. His companions mocked him, and he replied: "What could I do? This

202

animal escaped because his last hour, fixed by fate, was not yet come. Fate governs all, and the fisherman cannot overcome it more than another, nor can he catch fish, if fate is against him, even in the Tigris. The fish itself, even though dry, would not die, if it were the will of fate to preserve its life." The poet adds: "O man! why shouldst thou fear? If thy hour is not come, in vain would thy enemy rush against thee with his lance in rest: his arms and his feet would be tied by fate, and the arrow would be turned away, though in the hands of the most expert archer."

The spirit of Armenian poetry is neither despondent nor fatalistic. Its songs are of dawn, of spring, of sunrise, of struggle; not of sunset. And perhaps this clinging to hope and this desire to live is the only secret of the survival of the Armenian nation. Armenian poetry is the product of dwellers in a hill country. To them mountains, deep valleys, clear skies, running brooks are familiar every-day companions.

This brings us down to the Renaissance of Armenian literature which took place almost simultaneously in Russia and Turkey, but the field of modern Armenian literature is such a wide one that we cannot attempt an analysis of it here. There are, however, some examples of modern Armenian poetry in this volume.

Russian Era

The occupation of the Armenian provinces by Russia in 1828, with the attendant emigration of thousands from Persia and Turkey into Russian Armenia, strengthened the nation. National schools were soon opened, supported by the Armenians themselves. An Armenian Academy was established in Moscow in 1815 and a Seminary in Tiflis in 1826. Many Armenians went to Moscow and Petrograd, and also to foreign universities, especially to those of Germany, Switzerland, and France. The educational revival produced a new era, and a new Armenian literature came into being. Many Armenian newspapers and reviews were founded and published in different places. Tiflis was the centre of the literature and learning of Russian Armenia. A similar revival of letters occurred in Turkish Armenia. In 1860 a national and ecclesiastical constitution was granted to the Armenians in Turkey. For Turkish Armenians the literary centers were Constantinople and Smyrna. In the latter city, good work was done in translating western classics, but Constantinople was the chief seat of Armenian culture in Turkey. Thus Armenian literature became divided into two branches—Russian Armenian and Turkish Armenian—each of which has its own peculiarities of language, style, and tone. It was poetry that first burst into bloom and reached maturity soonest. At first the motifs of the poems were mainly national. The imagination of the poets was kindled by the past, present, and future of Armenia, its sufferings, its national beauty, its shortcomings. They looked forward to a national regeneration. They were apostles of light, science, learning; and pointed out new paths of national salvation. The result of all this was the production of some beautiful national songs. These songs are not triumphant anthems like those of other countries; they are songs of suffering, but with a note of hope. Then Armenian poetry developed a truer relation with what had been created in literature and art, and the poets looked at things in a new way, and assumed new poetical forms. It combined poetry and imagination with passionate feeling for life and truth. Some of the poems of this period are of exquisite workmanship, breathing the very spirit of the time.

As we have said, Armenian poetry of the nineteenth century is so full of merit and of such intense interest that it would be impossible to do it justice without writing at great length. We have already exhausted the space at our disposal, and hope to devote a separate work to it.

Persian and Arabic poetry are things of the past, but Armenian poetry, like the Armenian nation, has an unquenchable vitality, ever advancing towards new horizons, and soaring to loftier heights.

www.ingramcontent.com/pod-product-compliance
Lightning Source LLC
Chambersburg PA
CBHW020510100426

42813CB00030B/3191/J